Grace & GUTS

He Is Our Strength !

Shannon Terry

Psalm 18

"For every woman who has experienced betrayal, loneliness, uncertainty, anger or Satan's defeat and desires a better way, this book is for you! With a heart of joy and a love for God's Word, Shannon courageously confronts tough topics. Who hasn't been betrayed? Lonely? Angry? Uncertain? Insecure? Chapter by chapter, Shannon shines God's light and insights into the enemy's attempts to rob us of the Truth and the Life. Warning: this book takes guts and honest introspection, but you will return to its pages for more, and readily share it with friends."

—**Cheryl Roland**, Women's Director,
NE Indiana District Church of the Nazarene

"Shannon Perry's insight into the needs of women is a remarkable testament to how much we all struggle with the very same things. From loneliness to the temptation to people-please, Shannon helps us see that in the end, God has answers for all of our difficulties. There is no doubt you'll find your feelings about life staring back at you in the pages of this book, but when you turn the page you will find hope about how to tackle it, one day at a time."

—**Rene Gutteridge**, award-winning, best-selling author
of 24 multi-genre novels, one of which became a
popular Hallmark movie, www.renegutteridge.com

"*Grace and Guts* is a practical and powerful book and Shannon Perry's personal stories are wonderfully witty and relatable.

Prepare for your Christian walk to be illuminated, for your heart to be touched, and for your smile to return!"

—**Anita Higman**, Award-winning
and best-selling author of 47 books

"Drawing from adversities she has faced in life, Shannon uses Biblical insights and wit to help you overcome life's most difficult and painful challenges. You'll find *Grace and Guts* to be an enjoyable, inspirational read that will help you grow closer to God."

—**Arline Bell**, Senior Director of Programming, NRB TV

"Shannon Perry draws us into real life issues many of us have journeyed or are currently going through. Her transparency and authenticity shines as she tells her own personal stories. Of course, it wouldn't be Shannon without the thread of humor that makes you smile. *Grace and Guts* helps us find the grace we need to deal with difficult and painful situations. Shannon offers us a way to see God in the midst of all our circumstances."

—**Lynda Zelenka**, Associate Pastor, Foundry Church,
Houston, Texas, and Executive Director, Cy-Hope Inc.

"*Grace and Guts* is exactly what our hurting world needs right now. We are overwhelmed with negative thoughts and emotions through news, culture, social media and more. Shannon's insightful study ignites the belief that healing through God's grace will strengthen me into a warrior of the faith ready to believe, live and share Christ deeper every day."

—**Marsha Lambeth**, 100.7 FM, KKHT Program
Director/Salem Houston Production Director

Grace & GUTS

Strategies for Living a Knock-Out Life

SHANNON PERRY

NASHVILLE

NEW YORK • LONDON • MELBOURNE • VANCOUVER

Grace & GUTS
Strategies for Living a Knock-Out Life

© 2019 SHANNON PERRY

Published in New York, New York, by Morgan James Publishing. Morgan James is a trademark of Morgan James, LLC. www.MorganJamesPublishing.com

The Morgan James Speakers Group can bring authors to your live event. For more information or to book an event visit The Morgan James Speakers Group at www.TheMorganJamesSpeakersGroup.com.

ISBN 978-1-64279-045-0 paperback
ISBN 978-1-64279-046-7 eBook
Library of Congress Control Number: 2018939400

Cover Design by:
Rachel Lopez
www.r2cdesign.com

Interior Design by:
Bonnie Bushman
The Whole Caboodle Graphic Design

In an effort to support local communities, raise awareness and funds, Morgan James Publishing donates a percentage of all book sales for the life of each book to Habitat for Humanity Peninsula and Greater Williamsburg.

Get involved today! Visit
www.MorganJamesBuilds.com

DEDICATION

For Gina Adams,
Your guts and grace are an endless inspiration.

For Mom,
You won the final round with
the epitome of grace and guts!
Thank you for your final gift.

TABLE OF CONTENTS

ACKNOWLEDGMENTS

Thank you to my fearless editing team: Gina Adams, Sarah Benefiel, and Kristina Lewis.

Special thanks to Sarah Hall Photography and Design for the cover photo.

INTRODUCTION

Ministry is far from stages, lights and autographs. I'm not qualified for ministry because I'm perfect or because I have all of the answers. All that qualifies me to do ministry is Jesus Christ. With His help, I'm learning to fight life's battles alongside people like you.

After hearing from thousands of women, I have found it fascinating that despite our age, culture, denomination or season of life, we all struggle in similar areas. We are often hurled into the boxing ring of life and sucker punches are thrown our way that attempt to knock us down for the count. The good news? We have a knockout punch that wins every time—the power of God's Word.

In the few years that led to writing this book, I was thrown into a ring I neither wanted nor believed I needed. I watched my best friend, my mom, battle cancer. During those same years, my Dad was diagnosed with cancer—not once, but twice. My son and only child was deployed to serve his country overseas. My mom eventually won her battle and went to Heaven.

I would like to say I gladly entered the ring and fought those years courageously. I did not. I tried to bargain, plead, cry and fight to get out of that ring. Each time I attempted my escape, I hit the ropes and bounced right back onto the floor. I came to the conclusion that I had to go all nine rounds if I wanted to taste victory. I would also need two things for the win: grace and guts.

It takes grace to fight God's way. It takes guts to do it.

When we're stubborn, we often try a lot of things before we agree to God's way. In my case, I wanted to show God why my way was best. I silently hoped that if I prayed enough and got others to pray, He would somehow see that things needed to go *my* way.

I learned He listened to those prayers. I learned He answered. I also learned that prayer changed me, but did not always change my situation.

In *Grace and Guts*, we will learn Biblical strategies for throwing the knockout punch that helps us win the fight, no matter what we're facing.

If you have read any of my books or attended my conferences, you know that humor is one way I have managed to successfully handle trials. Some days I didn't want to laugh, so the funny stories in the book are meant to remind you to laugh in the ring.

If it feels like you're up against the ropes and are ready to deliver a knockout punch for the win in the areas where you're hit the hardest, this book is for you.

—Shannon

Chapter 1

THE GRACE AND GUTS TO CONQUER EXHAUSTION

How to Care for Yourself as You Care for Others

It was a Monday morning, and I had just returned to my home in Texas after a speaking engagement in Kentucky. I had slept little over the weekend and craved some much-needed rest. I found a lounge chair next to the pond behind my barn and nestled into my hiding place. No sooner did I find my peace than my neighbor found his Weed Eater. "Doesn't anyone know what quiet means anymore?" I mumbled and covered my ears to block the irritating buzz of the grass hacker.

I left my hiding place behind the barn and moved to our upstairs game room. As soon as I sat down on the couch, my husband called for me up the stairs. I would like to tell you I answered. I didn't. I sat very quiet knowing that if he really needed me, he would climb the stairs. He didn't, and I was glad. I didn't want to be found. I just wanted to REST!

We've all been there. We're exhausted and have nothing left to give. If we tried, it would be bad at best. We may even attempt to energize ourselves in less than desirable ways. When I need rejuvenation, I sometimes go shopping and eat Mexican food. One leaves me broke and the other leaves me bloated. Afterwards, I feel worse and have nothing left to give because I'm irritated *and* tired.

At times I have wondered what it would be like to live in a world where no one needs anything from me. Short of taking a vacation from life for a day, or hallelujah, a week, it's seemingly impossible. My dad needs me more now that Mom is in Heaven, my animals need me to feed them because they don't have thumbs, and my husband needs me for…where do I start? I'm found via Facetime or Facebook, but I don't want to "face" anything. I just want to rest. Can you identify? Jesus understands.

Jesus needed rest and at times even needed to be away from people. If we think WE are in demand, imagine how Jesus felt! He couldn't take a step without multitudes needing Him. Multitude, by definition, is a large number of people. If it were up to the multitudes, Jesus would have been busy day and night meeting their needs. After all, they wanted *what* they wanted *when* they wanted it. Sound familiar?

Since Jesus is our model, we have the freedom to follow His example because He followed His Heavenly Father. Genesis 2:2 says that "By the seventh day God had finished the work he had been doing; so on the seventh day He rested from all his work." Did God NEED rest? Hardly. He's omnipotent and has all power. Isaiah 40:28 reminds us that "The everlasting God, the Lord, the creator of the earth neither faints nor grows weary." He simply stopped. On purpose.

Many of us are so busy with what we think we "should" be doing that we don't take the time to stop, or rest, and consider why we are doing WHAT we're doing.

As I travel the country, I ask every congregation a question. "How many of you know what God's purpose is for this season of your life?" I can tell you that less than ten percent of the audience usually raises their hand.

Do you want to find the same rest that Jesus found on earth? Know your purpose, and you will. From the time that Jesus was born until the time He ascended into Heaven, Jesus knew His purpose, and He never lost His focus. He did only those things that He knew He was meant to do, and He let the rest of the world's demands go unmet. You mean Jesus used the word "no"? Absolutely. He knew the word "no" was a complete sentence.

Many of us have difficulty saying "no" because we're afraid of offending others. The next time you fear saying "no," think about Jesus. He wasn't afraid to offend man, but He never wanted to offend His Father. Jesus knew His purpose and He let nothing distract Him from that purpose. When we know

God's purpose for the season *we* are in, we can be at peace with saying "no." How can we find our purpose? We ask. It's that simple. We won't know the voice of God and what He wants for our life unless we schedule time alone with Him and ask what He desires for us.

So if it's that simple, why do we stay stressed and exhausted? Most of the time, we are battling the ability to lay boundaries. Guilt, doubt, uncertainty and fear attach themselves to us like a blood-sucking leech and our minds are drained while our bodies follow suit. Some days, we just can't get it all done. Other days, we don't even know what we're supposed to be doing. The process alone is exhausting and can make us want to quit. How can we lay boundaries to battle exhaustion? The following are some reminders.

THE GUTS TO WIN AGAINST EXHAUSTION:

1. **Begin each day with prayer.** Matthew 14 reminds us that Jesus found rest even when He was in great demand. After finding out that His cousin John the Baptist had been beheaded, Jesus got into a boat to be alone. In this same chapter, He feeds 5,000 people with two fish and five loaves of bread. After feeding the 5,000, He sends everyone away so He can be alone to pray. It's not long until He's needed again. The disciples meet a horrifying storm while sailing, so Jesus, awakened from His peaceful nap by His panicked brethren, calms the sea. As soon as the boat lands, Jesus is needed again by the multitude of people who are waiting on the shore to be healed.

Maybe you can identify with Jesus. The demands on you are endless and all you want is some time alone. Bills need to be paid, kids have to go to practice, friends need attention, calls need to be returned, the house is a wreck and dinner needs to be served. You know what needs to be done but you need some time to rest and re-energize so that you can get things done. Jesus could relate. He knew there were needs. He also knew He had to get alone with His Daddy (God) to receive the wisdom and strength to accomplish everything within His purpose. We need that same strength to meet needs within our own purpose.

While prayer is important to find the strength we need, we may find ourselves in a season where we feel too tired to even pray. We may not even know how or what to pray. Tears are all that come as we express our needs in exhaustion. Tears are a beautiful prayer that God understands. When we cry out and give God what we don't have in exchange for what He does have, something supernatural takes place.

God came to a lot of people who cried out in the Bible and He promises He will come to us, too. Psalm 72:12 says "He will deliver the needy who cry out." Not the self-sufficient, arrogant or the ones who have it all together, but the tired and needy. Psalm 3:4 says "To the Lord I cry out loud, and He answers me from His holy hill." Why does God pay close attention when we cry out? He sees our faith put into action and He moves on our behalf because we're trusting Him.

"Without faith it is impossible to please Him, for He who comes to God must believe that He is, and that He is a rewarder of those who seek Him" (Hebrews 11:6). God not only welcomes our cries for rest, He answers them. Give Him the "first fruits" of your time and He *will* answer your prayers for rest according to Exodus 33:14: "My presence shall go with you, and I will give you rest."

2. **Remain in God's timing**. Many times we're exhausted simply because we are acting outside of God's will. We're striving to do something that's not in His timing or purpose for us, or we feel pressured to "keep up" with what others are doing. God will give us what we need to fulfill the plan He has for us in every season of life. Our job is to find out what that plan is, and then execute it. Too many times, we allow fear, doubt, insecurity or our own stubborn ways to interfere with His plan for us. Exhaustion is the result when we fight God. Today, get into agreement with what God has for your life and allow Him to direct your path. He knows where you're going and how to get you there.

3. **Be aware of distractions**. Distractions are exhausting and come in all forms. From construction in traffic to hurtful words that ruin our day, distractions can divert us from rest and purpose. I know. One day I went to a doctor's visit with my dad and the nurse asked Dad if his "wife" would be joining him in the exam room. I quickly let the nurse know that his "daughter" would

remain in the waiting room. That same day, I drove through to get ice cream and was offered a "senior" discount. When the girl at the window saw the look on my face, she quickly added, "I mean, not that you qualify for the senior discount." Too late. My day had been damaged and so had my pride. Fortunately, I recognized the distraction and refused to allow those words to stop me from my purpose. I went back to my office, applied additional moisturizer and got back to my purpose—writing this book!

4. **Limit your time on social media**. I use social media on a daily basis and am in favor of many of its uses. Unfortunately, social media can steal the time we spend with Jesus. I know I'm guilty. Many mornings, I have found myself checking Facebook before I check "THE" book. Set a time limit on your social media and honor it. If you use it for business, refuse the temptation to read everyone's update until you have completed your tasks.

Inaccurate views from social media can also add to our exhaustion. When we're already tired and then read how "wonderful" everyone else is doing based on the posts they're making, more of our energy is often depleted. May I give you this simple reminder about social media? It's easy to post great things about life, however, few of us post when we've just screamed at our kids or been rude to a friend. Social media can also make us angry or upset, so spend the time you would normally devote to social media getting some much-needed rest. If reading helps you relax, grab the Bible and fill your heart and mind with God's "posts."

5. **Know your limits and take care of yourself**. Many of us were taught to be caretakers of others, but we have difficulty taking care of ourselves. Not only is taking care of ourselves acceptable, God expects us to oversee our health because we are the temple where He resides. (I Corinthians 6:19). Exhaustion has been linked to heart disease as well as other illnesses, so beware of the following signs that indicate you may be exhausted (Source: dailyburn.com):

- *Dry lips*. If your lips are cracked, your skin is scaly and you're suffering from frequent headaches, dehydration may be to blame. Doctors say to be sufficiently hydrated, we must drink water until our urine is clear.

- *Inability to concentrate*. When your mind is fuzzy, you may need more sleep. Our bodies use sleep to stabilize chemical imbalances, as well as to refresh areas of the brain that control mood and behavior. Go to bed at the same time every night and aim for getting the eight hours of sleep that most doctors recommend. Let others know you will not be disturbed after you go to bed and be disciplined enough to keep your routine. If you have difficulty falling asleep, keep a gratitude journal by your bed and write down ALL of the things that blessed you that day. Prayer is another peaceful way to relax your mind as you drift off to sleep.

- *You lack the will or drive to exercise.* One night of lost sleep can lead to weeks of missed workouts and unhealthy meals. Keep a weekly exercise program as part of your self-care regime. Begin by walking twenty minutes a day and then increase your exercise as your doctor sees fit.
- *You eat more junk food than usual.* The more exhausted you are, the more you crave high-fat, high-carb food. Reach for a banana instead of a bag of chips.
- *Your sleep patterns are unstable.* Decrease stimulation thirty minutes before bedtime by shutting down your phone and any other electrical devices.

God modeled the value of rest long before health officials knew of its importance. When we rest in God's truths and model our life after His example, we enter physical, emotional and spiritual rest that only He can give. So go ahead…and just rest.

Chapter 2

THE GRACE AND GUTS
TO HANDLE BETRAYAL

*Staying Off the Ropes when
You're Hit with a Sucker Punch*

couldn't believe my eyes as I read the Facebook post. A "friend" had taken an idea that she watched me craft for months and made it her own. In the comments below the post, another "friend" encouraged the idea, knowing it was originally mine. "Delete, delete, please delete!" I couldn't delete the post, and I couldn't delete the pain that washed over me as I stared at my computer screen.

I stepped off stage after a conference one night and a lady came up to me and whispered, "May I speak to you?" We walked outside and between waves of tears, she described the affair. "This is not just any affair. My husband slept with another man."

Betrayal. If you are over the age of one, something has probably been unfairly taken from you. Betrayal robs us of security and leaves us broken and lost. We trust a friend with facts that are soon twisted and grossly displayed for others to dissect. We pledge a covenant with God and man to find that man doesn't care to keep his part of the agreement.

Jesus understood the sting of betrayal. He was betrayed to death.

Jesus loved his disciple Judas and shared life-changing moments with him. Unfortunately, Judas surrendered to Satan, betrayed Jesus to his murderers and became one of the most hated humans in history. In John 13:18, Jesus says, "Even my own familiar friend in whom I trusted, who ate my bread, has lifted up his heel against me." Jesus must have been devastated knowing someone He had loved so deeply could betray Him so cheaply. Can you relate?

Interestingly, Jesus calls Judas His "friend" in Matthew 26:50. He wasn't bitter or angry toward Judas. He showed Him grace. How can we show grace to someone who throws away our trust like trash? The same way Jesus did. Forgive. When we do, we lay down our right to be God and let Him handle our offender.

I often hear people say they want to forgive but "can't." Could it be that we struggle to forgive because we lack a clear understanding of what forgiveness looks like?

I was perusing *Focus on the Family's* website recently, and found a wonderful article about forgiveness. The next time you struggle to forgive your offender, consider the following descriptions of forgiveness:

***Forgiveness does not mean we lack boundaries.** As we forgive, we maintain healthy boundaries. Our offender should continue to be held accountable for their actions or lack thereof.

***Forgiveness is allowing God to be the arbiter of justice.** When we transfer the right of revenge to God, we are telling Him we trust Him to handle the situation.

Recently, I paid for an item and walked out of the store only to be chased down by a security guard in the parking lot. When I asked why he was following me, he yelled, "Step back into the store ma'am!" As I stepped inside, every eye was on me. Horribly embarrassed, I removed all items from my bag. Undoubtedly, the security tag had been left on an item I purchased, and they believed I had stolen it. Once I showed the saleslady my receipt which proved I paid for the merchandise, she profusely apologized, as did the security guard. At that moment I had to make a decision. My flesh wanted to say, "Really, Barney Fife?" My spirit told me to let it go. I've found that God is a great teacher when we trust Him with the details.

***Forgiveness does not mean we have to be a victim.** Forgiveness is not a ticket for someone to walk on us. God designed us to be victors, not victims.

*Forgiveness is a progressive journey, not a single decision.** Turning our betrayer over to God may have to occur many times before we are free. It will be worth it!

*Forgiveness does not always mean we maintain a relationship with our perpetrator.** When betrayal occurs, a relationship is altered. Paul advises that we should live in peace with men as much as possible. There are times, however, that reconciliation is not helpful nor possible. If our betrayer repents by changing their actions, we may consider saving the relationship. If we do, we must take time to make sure acts of repentance are both genuine and lasting. If the relationship is saved, avoid throwing up an offense from the past. This may make you feel good temporarily, but can do great damage to an already fragile relationship.

*Forgiveness does not mean we deny reality or ignore recurring offenses.** Some people are mean-spirited and do not want to change. We need to stop expecting "gallon-sized" behavior from "pint-sized" people. Change your expectations and responses to those in your life who continually offend. Not doing so continues to set us up as victims.

*If our offender does not repent, we must still forgive.** When we wait for our perpetrator to apologize and take on the responsibility for their offense, we place the power in their hands. Forgiveness is about our attitude, not their action. Choose to forgive and release them to God so that there is no barrier between you and Him.

*We do not need to tell our offender we forgive them when they have not asked for forgiveness.** This can be a form of manipulation and an attempt to make our perpetrator feel guilty.

*Forgiveness offered out of fear or manipulation is not sincere forgiveness. The Bible says "perfect love casts out fear." If forced to forgive, remind your offender, "I will continue to pray and actively seek God's help to make my heart pure in this situation."

*Forgiveness does not mean we forget. When the pain of past hurts are triggered, thank God for the forgiveness and healing He provides in your broken places.

There is no "secret formula" for avoiding betrayal, but God's Word reminds us that "we will know them by their fruit." If someone says they're an apple tree but oranges are falling off their tree, guess what? They're an orange tree! People can tell us anything, but we are responsible for examining the fruit of their lives by watching their actions. We can increase the likelihood of avoiding people who exhibit toxic behavior when we test their actions against God's Word. We can love and pray for those with "rotten fruit," but we do NOT have to form intimate relationships with them.

We must also keep our hearts clean. Psalm 51:10 says, "Create in me a clean heart, oh God, and renew a right spirit within me." Your heart is the gate to your life, so be discerning about who you allow through the gate. Give relationships time before sharing too much of yourself. When something "doesn't seem quite right," pay attention to the "flags." Ask God for discernment and follow His instruction about who to allow into your life.

I have a lot of acquaintances and some great friends. Then there is my inner circle. These are the people I share my heart with because they have proven they are trustworthy. They're not perfect, but they are priceless. They pray for me when I'm broken, celebrate my successes, have no hidden agendas and challenge me with truth. I am grateful every day that they came through my gate.

When we're betrayed by someone we've allowed through our gate, it can be devastating. We trust someone with intimate details of our life only to find that they steal our trust and sell it for free. It can shut us down emotionally. How can we possibly move forward and overcome the devastation of betrayal? The following may be helpful:

THE GUTS TO BEAT BETRAYAL:

1. **Put limits on your thoughts.** It's easy to rehearse betrayal with ourselves and others. While it's important to acknowledge and accept that you've been betrayed, don't allow yourself to re-run the scene of the betrayal through your mind more than three times. When tempted, stop and pray. Ask God to remove the thoughts of how you've been wronged and all of the emotions that go with those thoughts.

2. **Look for patterns of behavior.** Unfortunately, some do not know what it looks like to be loyal and they repeat hurtful behaviors in all of their relationships. While it does not lessen the pain we feel, we can be aware of patterns in those who betray us and avoid making the same mistakes in future relationships.

3. **Find any positive behavior pattern and praise those.** This is tough. When someone has betrayed us, our hurting heart does not "feel" like praising the one who hurt us. Identifying and acknowledging positive behavior patterns will yank roots of bitterness out of our lives and allow us to heal from betrayal so that we don't carry hurt back into that relationship or relationships that follow.

4. **Give grace.** Don't shut the book. When someone hurts us, we need to find the guts to question why the betrayal occurred. If the deception was deliberate, you will more than likely not get a direct answer from the one who's betrayed you. Give grace, forgive and learn from the experience. If their betrayal was negligent and they wish to restore the relationship, forgive and extend restoration. Forgiveness does not mean you accept what they did or that the relationship will be restored immediately. Healing takes time. Healing may also occur in different ways and at different levels than you expected. Let God be God and take the lead on how your relationship will be restored.

5. **Be honest with the one who has hurt you.** Express your feelings of disappointment and hurt. Let your offender know you are choosing to give grace if you give the relationship another chance. Refuse to rehearse the offense. Remember, there is no "perfect" relationship because there are no "perfect" people. Trust God to be the vindicator and healer in every area that is damaged.

6. **Use wisdom.** If a "friend" betrays you and refuses to acknowledge their contribution to the demise of the friendship, then your "friendship" is a one-way street. Friendship is built on honesty. When truth is absent, it's impossible to nourish a Godly friendship because He is truth and in Him "there is no darkness." Forgive, but walk away if the foundation of your friendship is built on lies, deception or manipulation. God has better for you. Just like my "friends" on Facebook, I love and forgive them, but I now trust others with my ideas.

If you've been betrayed, you can begin again. Forgive your offender, let God heal your heart, then guard your gate. Ask God to bring those who don't just tolerate you, but celebrate you the way He does.

Chapter 3

THE GRACE AND GUTS TO CRUSH INSECURITY AND INFERIORITY

*Championing Self-Esteem,
Self-Worth and Confidence*

had just booked three exciting dates in one week, and I was thrilled. I felt confident, excited about what God was doing in the ministry and grateful He had chosen *me* to be the speaker for each event. Nothing could steal my joy. Nothing... except a magazine article from another speaker.

The more I read, the more I sighed. "This" speaker was booking *seven* dates a week. "This" speaker was going on a tour I would love to be on. "This" speaker had just finished recording an interview on a radio show that I *still* hadn't been on. "This... speaker..."

I turned and stared out the window. "Why couldn't *I* book seven dates a week? Why couldn't *I* be interviewed on that show? Am *I* not good enough?"

Inferiority. It convinces us we're "less" than others and is frequently accompanied by comparison. Comparison gives inferiority permission to make us believe we will never measure up. Inferiority lies, makes us want to quit, and leaves us feeling that we are on the outside of every circle we long to be in. It devours our faith.

Moses understood inferiority. When God asked Moses to approach Pharaoh, Moses responded, "Who am *I* that I should go to Pharaoh and bring the Israelites out of Egypt?" (Exodus 3:11). Isn't that something? God speaks **directly** to Moses and all he can squeak out is a response FILLED with inferiority! We may be surprised by Moses' behavior, but aren't we like him at times? I'm certainly guilty.

When I realized that God was preparing me to be a speaker, I gave every excuse I could think of to convince Him that He had chosen the wrong girl. "Have you HEARD my voice Lord? I talk like I'm six years old!" When I call to make airline reservations, the agent usually asks if my mom will be traveling with me because I sound so young.

I gave every excuse that I could think of to convince God and others that I am not a speaker. None of them worked. When I finally surrendered to do my first speaking engagement there were 1,000 women in attendance. You talk about feeling inferior! I wanted to RUN out of that room.

I was escorted to the front of the ballroom where I sat nervously terrified until it was time for me to speak. When I walked onto the platform, it comforted me to see that all the women were smiling. All… but one.

It's amazing to me that 999 women in that room were smiling and I managed to lock eyes with the one who was not. Not only was she frowning, she stared me up… and… down… and up… and down. Panic raced through me and I knew this could mean only one thing: She. Hates. Me.

By the grace of God, I finished speaking and received a standing ovation. I exited the stage like my pants were on fire and headed to my product table. When I reached the back of the room, I was stunned to find long lines of people waiting to purchase my products. Leading the way was the very lady who had frowned during my entire presentation! She hugged me, told me how much my words had meant to her and purchased one of everything on my table.

I learned a valuable lesson that night. Living in inferiority often causes us to draw false conclusions and destroys "God moments" in our life.

God has grown my confidence since that first speaking engagement. He has shown me that He *chose* this "six-year-old voice" to make a difference in the lives of others. From TV to radio and events all around the United States, God has not been stopped by what I felt were my limits. If we will allow Him, God loves to use the very thing that makes us feel the most inferior.

Maybe you can identify with how I was feeling during my first speaking engagement. Your neighbor's house is immaculate, her kids are well-behaved, and her nails are perfectly manicured. Meanwhile, you're struggling to find your keys under yesterday's laundry and feel like a savage living next to Miss America. I get it.

I remember the time I was told to bring a bag of potatoes to work because we were serving baked potatoes for our staff. I did exactly as requested. No one told me they had to be baked! You should have seen the looks I got from some of my colleagues when I walked in carrying that brown net filled with uncooked potatoes. I still laugh about it and often blame my feelings of inferiority as a cook on that traumatizing event.

Maybe it's not cooking but Bible studies that leave you feeling inferior. You have great confidence at work, but when you're asked to teach a Bible study, you panic. When you finally agree, you're petrified to find "Martha of Bible Study Marathons" has decided to attend your class. Not only has she taught Bible studies, she's written and published them! You sink in your chair, smile your best fake smile and pray that you can find Psalms when you open your Bible.

The opportunity to feel inferior is everywhere, so how do we face it with grace? Understanding what drives us to feel inferior is a good place to start.

Inferiority lies to us. It says our flaws outweigh our strengths. We may have beautiful hair, gorgeous eyes and look great in our new shoes, but all we see are thighs when we look in the mirror. The longer we stare, the more of them we see. Eventually we see nothing else on our body but thighs and suddenly we're the ugliest woman in the world, no one wants to be our friend, and we need a cookie!

The longer we glare at our perceived imperfections, the more exaggerated they become. The next time inferiority invades your vision, try focusing on the good in your situation. After all, there are people who wish they could stand to see their thighs in the mirror, but they are bound to a wheelchair. Others will never see their thighs because they're blind.

My dad has always said that "Eating carrots will kill you." While he's joking, and I've never eaten a carrot because I don't like many vegetables, I can tell you that ingesting inferiority can kill your ability to have a healthy relationship with others.

If you're struggling with inferiority today, allow God to set you free as you find the guts to break loose.

THE GUTS TO DEFEAT INFERIORITY:

1. **Courageously explore your root of inferiority.** Were you neglected, bullied or criticized as a child? Maybe inferiority developed as an adult and you feel like you can never live up to anyone's expectations, including your own.

2. **Be aware of how inferiority is impacting your life.** When we feel less than others, we often settle for unhealthy relationships. We may also isolate ourselves, become controlling, refuse compliments or find it difficult to trust others. Indulging in compulsive behaviors that harm us may also be common if we're not aware of how we allow feelings of inferiority to affect our behavior.

3. **Examine the people you are around when you feel inferior.** Do you feel inferior to attractive people,

wealthy people or those you believe are more talented than you?

4. **Challenge your thinking.** After identifying who you are around when you feel inferior, develop five reasons that you do not need to feel inferior around them. Do they have your family values? Your sense of humor? Your peace in the middle of stress? One way I have found to help defeat inferiority is to decide what you would NOT trade with another person. It's amazing how blessed we are when we approach inferiority from this angle.

5. **Remember that everyone has something they'd like to change.** I have NEVER spoken to a woman who believes she's perfect. Actually, most of us are quick to reveal our flaws and conceal our strengths. When I was young and felt inferior about my looks, my mom would always say, "She may be beautiful, but there will always be someone in the world even more beautiful." She was right. There will always be someone more talented, wealthier, better at cooking, more organized, etc.

6. **Focus on your strengths.** When we stop striving to be like others and appreciate the uniqueness God gives us, we can be freed from inferiority. Being inspired by others is fine, but operating in the unique personality, gifts, and strengths God gives us is where we'll find freedom. Stay focused on doing what it takes to improve *your* strengths.

7. **Stay in God's will for you.** When we have a root of inferiority, we obsess over what others think about us.

When we do, we often focus on what others think we should do, and we don't focus on God's will for our life. If you don't know His will, ask. He longs for you to live in the center of His purpose for your life. One thing we should never have to work at is being ourselves. That's the joy of being uniquely YOU!

8. **Live from your strengths.** When I'm signing books at my table, I often say "tell me about you." Nearly everyone will tell me about their role. "I'm a mom, wife, student, etc." Few can answer my next question. "What are you good at doing?" They can tell me what they *enjoy* doing, but their friends usually have to tell me their strengths. Challenge yourself to make a list of your strengths. When you get into "comparison mode," focus on that list. It is not about being better than someone else. It's about being the best YOU that God created. When we compare ourselves to others, we can come up with a never-ending list of how we don't measure up. The truth is, we *can't* compare ourselves to others because God did not design us to run THEIR race. Run YOUR race and you won't have time to focus on what others are doing.

9. **Practice acceptance.** "When I lose weight, I'll be happy. When I'm married, I'll be happy. When I'm single, I'll be happy…" While these may sound great temporarily, they do not heal our root of inferiority. Instead of longing for what you don't have, think, "When I accept what God has for me, I'll be happy."

When we are confident that we are right where He wants us to be, inferiority flees.

10. **Tame your self-deprecating tongue.** I'm convinced there is a book that I have yet to put my hands on, but every woman has read it. In this book, permission is given to every woman to talk down to herself. It gives her permission to say things like "You're so stupid," or "You're ugly." She can only say these things to herself, however, because she would NEVER say them to anyone else.

    Does that apply to you, sweet friend? If so, make an agreement between you and God to STOP the negative talk. It not only hurts you, it hurts the Holy Spirit inside of you. He made you on purpose, with a purpose. When we talk down to ourselves, we are telling our Creator that He didn't do a good job. Replace the negative with truth today. Instead of telling yourself you're a failure because you didn't get the whole house cleaned, focus on the fact that you made the bed and did a load of laundry. If you had a goal to lose ten pounds but you've only lost five, congratulate yourself. That's five pounds you don't have to carry like you did before you lost them.

11. **Ask God to remove the labels that you were not made to wear.** In Isaiah 43, God reminds us that He has called us by name and we are His. We do not belong to ourselves so we don't get to label ourselves. The only labels we get to wear once we receive Jesus as

our Savior are those He places on us: Forgiven, secure, capable, valuable, loved. Those other labels you used to wear no longer fit you because you have been bought with the highest price God could ever pay.

The next time inferiority rears its horrible head, take out your sword and cut its head off. Hebrews 4:12 says, "The word of God is quick, and powerful, and sharper than any two-edged sword, piercing even to the dividing asunder of soul and spirit and of the joints and marrow, and is a discerner of the thoughts and intents of the heart." Slay the lies you hear with truth:

"I am the body of Christ and Satan has no power over me. For I overcome evil with good" (I Corinthians 12:27; Romans 12:21).

"I will fear no evil for thou are with me Lord, your Word and your Spirit they comfort me" (Psalm 23:4).

"No weapon formed against me shall prosper, for my righteousness is of the Lord. But whatever I do will prosper for I'm like a tree that's planted by the water of life" (Isaiah 54:17; Psalm 1:3).

"Christ has redeemed me from the curse of the law. Christ has redeemed me from poverty, from sickness and from spiritual death" (Galatians 3:13; Deuteronomy 28:15-68).

"The blessing of Abraham has come upon me through Jesus Christ and therefore whatever I do will prosper" (Galatians 3:14).

"I can do all things through Christ who strengthens me. There is nothing I cannot do through Christ for with God all things are possible" (Philippians 4:13; Matthew 19:26).

"I am the head and not the tail, above and not beneath" (Deuteronomy 28:13).

Chapter 4

THE GRACE AND GUTS TO OVERCOME FAITHLESSNESS AND FEAR

Clinching Victory in the Toughest Round

Where do you go when you want to be alone? I have two spots. One is in my barn and the other is my upstairs guest room.

Rarely does someone look for me upstairs, so my guest room is a perfect "get-away." I confess, there are times I doze off and mumble a string of senseless words when I lay down to pray. At other times, I don't even know *what* to pray. I vividly remember one of those times.

It had been a horrible day after our long visit to MD Anderson Cancer hospital. My mom was told there was nothing else they could do to treat her and hospice should be contacted. My son also called to let me know he would be deployed overseas and would possibly miss seeing my mom's final days. Both hits in one day seemed too much to bear.

Completely exhausted, I crawled upstairs to my guest room and flung myself across the bed. I cried until it felt like my guts would explode. WHY wouldn't God heal my mom? WHY did it feel like He was rejecting my desperate cries for healing? WHY wouldn't He do a miracle? WHY? WHY? WHY? Feeling faithless and hopeless, I threw myself head first into my pillow. All I could yell between sobs was, "Jesus!"

While this was *not* the first time I have prayed such a prayer, it *is* the first time I experienced what happened next.

With no warning, no flashing lights and no announcement, Jesus came into that room. I couldn't physically see Him, but I knew He was there. The peace that engulfed me is unexplainable and what happened next is unforgettable.

As if someone flipped a switch, my hysterical sobs turned to hilarious laughter. Not just the loud laughter I am known for, but an uncontrollable laughter that made no sense! I thought, "Shannon, this is crazy! If someone sees you, they will have you committed!" I had heard others talk about having a similar experience, but to be honest, I thought they might be "a fork and a knife short of a full place setting."

As I laughed between breaths, I knew God was doing a miracle. It wasn't for Mom. It was for me. I never heard an audible voice, just a soft whisper in my spirit. "I allowed you to have this experience tonight so that you could have a glimpse of the peace that your mom is going to experience when she is with me."

Immediately, I knew my mom would not be healed on this earth. I will never know why God chose not to heal her, but because of my experience in the guest room that night, I am at peace with not knowing. The God of the universe chose to step into my hurt, my heart and my home for that brief moment in time and visit *me!* Not only was my faith increased that night, I was reminded that I don't have to understand His ways. I just have to trust them. His visit is my forever reminder that He was in charge of mom's life from beginning to end. He is also in charge of yours and mine when we know Him as Savior.

Maybe you're facing a situation and find yourself asking, "Why?" If answers have disappeared and your faith has faded, the following can help reignite your faith.

1. **Speak the Word of God *out loud*.** Our brain is like a computer, storing all the information it receives. When we speak God's promises out loud, our mind records the truths it hears. As we repeat this process, His promises take root in our hearts and minds and eventually our actions will change based on our new beliefs.

2. **Know that your feelings of "faithlessness" do not change our Holy God's "faithfulness."** 2 Timothy 2:13 says, "If we are faithless, He remains faithful; He cannot deny Himself." God is faithful to us despite our *feelings* of faithlessness because He cannot go against His Word. His Word never changes based on feelings,

so on those days it feels like God is on vacation and forgot to pick you up, remember that He is strong enough to handle your doubts. He will never leave you, abandon you or give up on you. Your feelings don't determine His love for you. His death and resurrection do.

3. **Trust the facts, not your feelings.** Feelings are fickle and don't always speak truth. God's Word is unchanging and always speaks truth. Jesus said that His sheep know His voice and they follow Him (John 10:27-28). When life seems dark with no end in sight, we can still choose to trust Him. Choose to trust Him. Challenge your feelings with facts from God's Word. Unlike our feelings, His Word is a rock that never moves. Even when things turn out differently than we had planned, He still has plans to give us a "future and a hope" (Jeremiah 29:11).

THE GUTS TO SET BOUNDARIES WHEN WE FEEL FAITHLESS:

When we feel faithless, we may be tempted to quit on God, the church, Bible study and prayer. While turning to anything other than Christ may bring relief as a temporary fix, the results are just that—temporary. Find the "guts" to fight faithlessness when you build the following into your routine:

1. **Read your Bible**. Find passages that are promises for what you're walking through and MAKE THEM PERSONAL. Say the passage out loud and include

your name. For example: "Shannon, He will heal your broken heart, and He will bind up your wounds" (Psalm 147:3).

Next, write your promises on an index card, punch a hole in the cards and put them on a round ring. Carry that ring everywhere you go. When standing in the grocery line, or sitting in line at the bank, read the promises on that ring. Keep that ring of promises close by and memorize every promise made to you. Your feelings may not change right away, but your mind believes what you're saying. Eventually, your feelings will catch up.

2. **Spend time in prayer.** "Jesus" may be the only word you can say, but anything can happen when we speak His name. God does not need our fancy, religious prayers. He wants our honest, heart-felt prayers. He is never surprised by what we feel. He wants to meet us at the intersection of faithlessness and feelings to show us His faithfulness in the middle of our mess.

3. **Spend time with other believers**. The enemy loves to isolate us, especially when we feel faithless. I remember days when I felt entirely alone as Mom battled cancer. How grateful I was to have a group of believers I could call on to pray me through those days. A text, a call or a quick email from friends and family helped get me through the toughest days of that journey. Find those who will pray you through your "faithless" days. Ecclesiastes 4:9-10 reminds us that "Two are better than one... if one of them falls down, one can help

the other up. But pity the one who falls and has no one to help them up." If you cannot find a believer to hold you up, contact our office. We will stand in prayer with you.

Chapter 5

THE GRACE AND GUTS TO
DEFEAT PEOPLE-PLEASING

Throwing Insecurity, Insignificance
and Shame a Knock-Out Punch

For years, I sang solos in our church Christmas pageant. Now, our pageants were *anything* but typical. A caged lion was always rolled onto stage for the grand finale'. Lights flashed, the lion roared loudly and the audience would erupt in applause at the end of every performance. While the lion was cute, we were warned to keep our distance. He had been known to scar some hands through the open bars of his cage.

One year, I sang a solo prior to the lion's entrance. After I sang, I exited backstage through the black curtain and put my hands in front of me to feel my way down the dark hallway. Suddenly, I froze. A "growl" rang out behind me that stopped me in my tracks. It sounded very close, and it didn't sound happy. Unable to move, or see, I suddenly felt a warm sensation run down the back of my Biblical costume. Mr. Lion had relieved himself, and the smell was HORRIBLE! If he could have spoken to me in that moment, I'm quite sure he would have said, "You better back up, lady." Back up I did. I fluffed my costume dry, took a deep breath and ran back to the stage.

As I walked through the crowd of characters on stage, I wanted to giggle. One man waved his hand and whispered, "What is that smell?" I just grinned and whispered, "Me!" I smelled like a port-o-potty, and I made sure that I *never* turned my back to the audience. I was afraid they might think it was me, and not Mr. Lion, who soiled my threads.

Fearing what others think can be paralyzing. "What if they reject me? What if I'm not good enough? What if they laugh at me? What if? What if?" The "What if's" are a glue the enemy uses to keep us stuck in fear and insecurity. I know. For years, I worked overtime to be perfect because I desperately wanted people to accept me. What others thought of me became the air I breathed. If they approved of what I did, I was happy. If they didn't approve of me, I worked harder to "fix" me so they would. It took years to realize there are some people we will never please no matter how hard we try, and the rest will love us, despite our imperfections.

In her book *The Gifts of Imperfection*, Brene´ Brown writes, "Healthy striving is self-focused and asks 'How can I improve?' Perfectionism is other-focused and asks 'What will they think?'" While striving to improve ourselves is healthy, obsessing over other's opinions is disastrous. It is also displeasing to God. He wants first place in our lives and doesn't want to be put behind the opinion of others.

Since I have battled people-pleasing, I'd like to share what worked for me. **Putting the Holy Spirit first in every decision of my life is the ONLY thing that has helped me overcome people-pleasing.** When I learned to follow the Holy Spirit's lead, He honored my obedience and released me from the obligation, guilt, doubt and fear I faced when I felt I had disappointed others. While I still enjoy knowing that others are happy with my decisions, I no longer crumble when they disapprove. When I know I have prayed and followed the direction I received from God to the best of my ability, I leave the outcome to Him and go about life.

As you read this, you may be struggling with people-pleasing behaviors that derive from feelings of insecurity or insignificance. Maybe shame screams, "You will never be enough!" Shame speaks its own language and digs at the most tender parts of our heart. Shame is about who we believe we are as a person. It makes us feel invisible when someone overlooks us and screams, "You don't matter." When we feel shame, we're desperate for someone or some thing to blow enough air into our ever-deflated tank to keep us emotionally afloat one more day. The problem is, they can't.

While God created us for loving, healthy relationships, He never calls us to depend on the reassurance of others for our emotional stability. I Samuel 12:24 reminds us, "Only fear the Lord and serve HIM in truth with all your heart." When it comes down to what people think or what God thinks, we will never lose when we go with God.

If you are up against the ropes, and people-pleasing is threatening to knock you down, I pray that the following strategies bring victory into every fear-filled crevice of your heart as you fight to win this round.

1. **Remember that we all have insecurities.** It's been said that we would care a lot less about what others think about us if we realized how little time they spend thinking of us. Everyone has their own insecurities. When we believe we are the only one with insecurities, we're tempted to isolate ourselves. Be careful! Isolation breeds isolation. Enjoy getting to know others and remember that no one's opinion of you determines your eternal destiny. They're just not that powerful! It's much easier to worry less about the immediate when our eyes are on the eternal.

2. **People change their minds.** We can waste a lot of time altering ourselves to please others and then find they've changed their minds about what pleases them once we make changes. It's a never-ending battle.

    Hebrews 13:6 says, "The Lord is my helper, I will not fear. What can man do to me?" and Proverbs

29:25 reminds us that "The fear of man brings a snare." Fearing others can set them up to be an idol in our lives when we give away our right to think, feel and make decisions. We perceive others as more valuable than ourselves, and we may even value them more than God. We set man on a pedestal and sit God in the background. Sobering, isn't it? How many times have we become so afraid that we run from the very things God is asking of us because we are terrified of man? I know I qualify.

While everyone is entitled to their opinion, we are required to listen to one—God's. Excessive worry over what others think makes us wear ourselves out to gain someone's approval and then work tirelessly to keep it. It's exhausting, and it is not God-honoring. God wants us to seek His plan for our lives and follow it. The rest will fall into place.

3. **Remember that the people you surround yourself with can have a powerful influence over how you feel, think and behave.** Choose wisely.

4. **Evaluate your motives.** During one of my conferences, I talk about motives in the topic entitled "Goody Two Shoes." James 4:3 says, "You ask and do not receive because you ask with wrong motives." When we practice people-pleasing behaviors, we usually do things out of fear, obligation or guilt. When we are Holy Spirit-led, we do things because we want to please God and put His opinion first. Each time you

feel that sickening tug in your gut, ask yourself who you're trying to please.

5. **Surround yourself with those who maintain discipline in their lives.** Disciplined people strive to make good choices. Don't hang out with those who encourage you to shop if you are in credit card debt. Choose people who push you to make right decisions, even when it's difficult.

6. **Live by God's definition of success**. Too many times we allow what others are wearing, driving or doing determine where we are standing on the proverbial ladder of success. Unfortunately, if our heart isn't pretty, no house, car, or clothes can cover it up. God's Word reminds us that "Man looks on the outside, but God looks at the heart." When we "earn" the respect of others by the stuff of this world, it's meaningless. Don't get me wrong. Nice things are great when God blesses us with them. We just need to be sure that we chase the God who "refines" instead of the god of "finer things." Be a seeker of God's Kingdom first, and then "all these things will be added unto you."

7. **Always seek God's Kingdom**. Simply put, seek the things of God over what others think. Ask yourself questions such as "Where do I primarily put most of my energy? Do I spend more time reading God's Word to see what He thinks about what I'm doing or do I get on social media to see what others think? I know some who get upset if a certain number of people don't respond to their daily posts on Facebook. When we live

from a place of insecurity, we look for acceptance in all the wrong places.

We MUST get our identity and security in Jesus, or Satan will yank our "people-pleaser" chain until Jesus returns. God wants to heal every place in our heart that is reeling for the approval of others. Does that mean we stop caring about people? Absolutely not. Recently, a dear friend pulled me to the side and said: "I care about people, but not much about what they think." While we should always care about other's hearts, we must care about the heart of God above all others.

We all come from different experiences, backgrounds and ideas; therefore, some people may not like us. If you're struggling in the people-pleasing department today, help is on the way. Pray and ask God to give you the passion to follow His voice above the pressure and demands of others. Ask Him to fill your life with His approval, and overwhelm you with His acceptance. Strive to make Colossians 1:10 your life verse: "That you may walk in a manner worthy of the Lord, fully pleasing to Him and desiring to please Him above all things."

Chapter 6

THE GRACE AND GUTS TO DEMOLISH ADDICTION

Defeating a Deadly Competitor

t may come as a surprise that I've included this chapter. Addiction is often kept in "secret." Countless women have confided in me about their own addiction or of those they love. While Satan keeps truth in the dark, I've chosen to bring truth to light—much of which I've learned through personal experience.

Loving an addict can be terrifying and unpredictable. Their behavior crushes the heart and causes excruciating loneliness. If you have lived with it, you know what it looks like. If you have not lived with it, fall on your face and thank God that He has spared you.

Addiction is baffling, cunning, and according to statistics, 23.5 million Americans are addicts. That's approximately one in every ten Americans over the age of 12.

While I cannot be certain, I believe I'm safe to surmise that most of us have been touched by addiction in some way. Maybe you're the wife who hides in terror from a drunk husband or the mom whose meth-addicted child goes missing for days on end. Perhaps you're the wife who walks in insecurity and loneliness due to your husband's porn addiction. Maybe, the addict is you.

While I could write an entire book on addiction (and one day I might), there are boundaries that must be put into place when dealing with this difficult, arcane, and crazy-making disease. Without these boundaries in place, life becomes an endless path of crazy. I know.

One night when the addict in my life decided to go to a bar three miles from my home, I followed…on foot…in my pajamas! I walked because the addict had hidden my keys to deter me from following. At 1 A.M., I decided I would "fix" this problem once and for all and "make" the addict come to his senses.

In a long overcoat and winter hat, I trudged through the neighborhood. Dogs howled when I walked passed their yard. As cars approached, I ducked behind bushes so I wouldn't be seen. After all, someone might think I was crazy!

When I finally reached the bar, I peered through the thick yellow glass embedded in the door. Suddenly, I was distracted by the sound of motorcycles. I turned to find the "Hell's Angels" pulling into the parking lot.

As each got off their bike, they stared awkwardly. They obviously weren't staring at me as a recruit. They were staring at the pajamas hanging out from underneath my overcoat! The "Hell's Angels" were looking at *me* like *I* was crazy! At that moment, it hit me, *I am the one acting crazy!* I called for a ride home and went to bed. I made a vow to God and to myself that night that I would never do something like that again.

Though that was years ago, the lesson bears repeating: our behavior can be as crazy as the addict's behavior when we lack healthy boundaries. Our job, therefore, is to work on our *own* behavior and leave the addict in God's hands. Your life and sanity **can** be restored when the light of God's truth penetrates the darkness of addiction.

Some medical professionals identify addiction as a "disease" and those who live with or love an addict know how infectious their addiction can be if boundaries are not in place. When we "do" life with an addict, we may find:

1. Our every thought is consumed with their behavior and what they may or may not do next.
2. We are exhausted, watching the addict's physical, mental and emotional state deteriorate as they continue using their "drug" of choice. Eventually, we begin to deteriorate with the addict if we become obsessed with their wellness.
3. We grow angrier as the addict lies, manipulates or displays other unacceptable behavior.

4. We are misunderstood by others when we try to explain the chaos we're experiencing.

5. We grow frustrated when others make excuses for the addict or just "don't get it."

6. We feel like we're the crazy ones when blamed for the addiction.

7. We live in constant stress or fear of what the addict will do next.

8. We are told that lies are the truth and that everything is our fault.

9. We become hopeless as we run out of answers to "fix" the addict.

10. We question God and how He could allow something like this to happen.

While living with or loving an addict may feel impossible, there are answers. You can even "live well" as you face life with an addict. The pain of watching an addict destroy themselves is gut- wrenching, but our suffering can be lessened when we put truth into place.

If someone you love is an addict, prayerfully consider the following:

1. **You are not the cause of the addiction**. No matter how many times you are blamed for the addiction or how true the lies may sound, it is not your fault.

2. **Learn to separate the person from the addiction**. The "Dr. Jekyll, Mr. Hyde" complex is real, so agree to only talk with the man/woman that God created them

to be, not the addict who lies, manipulates, blames and rages.

3. **Your love alone cannot stop the addiction**. An addict's perception is warped, and all the love in the world does not change them. Only God's love and healing can deliver the addict.

4. **You can love the person and hate the addiction**. Addicts live in a compulsive state of shame. Addicts believe nothing is "right" about them; therefore, they sink deeper when we shame them. Avoid degradation. It will not benefit you or your addict in any way.

5. **Forgive yourself if you have acted in ungodly or unloving ways toward the addict**. None of us is born into this world with the skill set it takes to handle the complications of addiction.

6. **Addicts get help when they are ready to get help and not a moment sooner**. While the boundaries you set (discussed below) can help drive them to wanting help, it is ultimately the addict's choice. Continue praying for them and encouraging them to get the help they need but remember, it is ultimately their decision.

7. **Be diligent about the words you choose to believe from an addict**. Addicts lie to themselves about their addiction. As a result, they lie to those around them.

8. **Stop enabling the addict**. Lying for them, making excuses for them or running like crazy to keep the addict happy will not stop their addictive behavior. But it WILL destroy you.

9. **Do not allow shame to keep you hidden from truth**.
Find those who understand addiction and talk with
them. Do not try to make others understand addiction
if they are unable.

Remember that you can get healthy and have a life whether
your addict is using or not.

THE GUTS TO DRAW BOUNDARIES WITH ADDICTION:

*Don't be afraid to say "no".** We are not responsible for
the addict's reaction when we say "no," only our response to
their reaction.

*Never argue with the addict**. Walk away. If they are in
your home, find something else to do. Go to another room
and do something productive. If the addict follows you, leave
until you feel it's safe to return. Most importantly—do NOT
engage the addict when they are abusive. Addicts love to blame
others and take the focus off of themselves. Do NOT argue, talk
back or engage in any way. You will lose. Think of it as sticking
your hand in the mouth of an alligator. Nothing good can come
from it.

*Let go.** Nothing about the addict will change if you let go
of your controlling behavior. What will change, is you. Change
is like a mobile. When a baby has a mobile hanging over his
crib, the mobile shifts and moves each time the baby moves.
When we change, our emotional "mobile" shifts because the
weight of our focus is no longer on the addict, but on ourselves.
As a result, the addict must shift. Warning: Addicts don't like

change. They may do many things to get you "back in line." Stand strong. Doing what is best for you will save you and possibly your addict. Letting go does not mean you stop loving or caring for the addict. It means you guard your heart as God commands.

***Guard your heart and needs.** When you're flying, there's a reason they tell you to put your oxygen mask on first before coming to the assistance of others. If you can't breathe, both of you will die.

Dealing with an addict is difficult, and I would add impossible, if we do not have truthful and Biblical boundaries in place. Without boundaries, those who love addicts will fall apart. Proverbs 4:23 commands us to "guard our heart." This verse goes on to remind us that "everything we do flows from the heart." When our heart is left with no boundaries to protect it, our heart gets sick. As a result, the things that "flow from our heart" and, ultimately our lives, look nothing like Jesus.

How can we guard our heart when dealing with an addict? Here are some practical ways:

1. Stop spending money, buying alcohol, driving to drug deals, making excuses to friends or getting the addict out of jail. In essence, do not be a part of the addict's drug of choice. While the addict will not like these boundaries, you will like your newly found self-respect.

2. Determine the behaviors you deem unacceptable and the appropriate consequences.

3. Carry out your boundaries firmly. Nagging is one thing. Showing the addict you will carry through with your

boundaries is another. If the addict chooses to drink and drive, drive separate cars to any function you will attend together. You are not your addict's babysitter. You are a responsible adult taking care of yourself.

4. Lovingly tell the addict that you cannot be around them when they are using or exhibiting "addict" behavior. Setting boundaries requires firmness, not harshness.

5. Do not protect your addict from the natural consequences that occur as a result of their choices. You will only delay their healing.

6. No longer accept the blame that is placed on you for the addiction. Addiction is a condition that affects the brain. You didn't cause their brain to be wired this way, and you can't love them enough to unwire it. They need God's deliverance from the chains of addiction.

7. Seek help for yourself. Godly counselors trained in dealing with addiction are a great support when you feel alone. If you are unable to pay for professional services, "Celebrate Recovery" is offered at many churches and serves as a powerful tool for helping those living in or with addiction.

Perhaps you are unable to draw boundaries because *you* are the one struggling with addiction. There is hope for you. God's will is that you would be freed from every chain that binds you. Surrendering is key.

*Surrender your attempts to overcome addiction on your own. There are those who are equipped and ready to offer help when you're ready to receive it.

*Surrender the feeling that your life is not worth living. John 3:16 says Jesus loved you so much that He gave His very life for you. He's the one who will love you with an unfailing love. Run to Him.

*Surrender the guilt. You are deserving of a new life. Not because of what you have or haven't done, but because of what Jesus Christ has done for you at the cross.

*Surrender your weaknesses. There will be days that the fight against addiction is tough, even when you enter recovery. Don't give up. Jesus Christ is all the dependence you need to fight temptation. He knows what it feels like to be tempted when weak. He also knows how to give you the strength to conquer the temptation to relapse.

*Surrender your entire life to Jesus. In Job 16:21, Jesus "pleads with God as one pleads for a friend." No one will *ever* love you more or fight more for you to have victory over your addiction than Jesus.

Whether you are struggling with an addiction or live with or love an addict, there is hope. When we surrender to God's perfect will for our lives, we find the hope, peace and love that Jesus died to give.

Chapter 7

THE GRACE AND GUTS TO OVERPOWER LONELINESS

Going the Distance to Find Your Tribe

"I cried myself to sleep last night. No one knew, and it seemed no one really cared. I punched through every number on my cell phone but no one answered. I wanted somebody, anybody, to answer. I just needed a human connection, but it felt like the whole world was silent. If God really cared, wouldn't He let someone answer? Of course. God must not care either. Why am I even here? Who even cares that I'm here? God! Where. Are. You?"

Unfortunately, this story is a more common occurrence than we'd like to believe. Not only is it one that I have heard, I have lived it. I have felt so lonely that it seemed like I was the only one in the world who has EVER felt this feeling. Perhaps you can identify.

Being alone and being lonely are different. If you're like me, I *need* time alone every now and then. Loneliness is different. Loneliness leaves us feeling painfully disconnected from others. When we feel disconnected, it can seem like no one understands us, cares about or loves us. It may even feel impossible to *want* to connect, so we separate from others and our loneliness grows worse.

Loneliness doesn't typically develop overnight. It may evolve after a major life event, but it is usually the result of life experiences. Sometimes we remain lonely because we have childhood trauma and refuse to trust. Others of us feel separated and find it hard to be transparent. We may feel negatively about ourselves, so we shy away from relationships or have overbearing personalities that push people away. We may also feel sheer terror when loneliness sets in because we were abandoned as children.

When experiencing loneliness, we need guts to avoid making decisions that have destructive outcomes. An expensive vacation you can't afford may temporarily soothe your pain, but loneliness is sure to return like an unwelcomed houseguest when you resume your routine.

If we are functioning humans, we have a natural desire to connect with others. In Genesis 1, the first words God spoke is it's "not good" for man (woman) to be alone. It is by God's design that we have an innate need to be loved and to belong.

John 10:10 reminds us that Christ came so that we can "live life to the fullest," even when we face loneliness. When Paul was in a Roman jail, he faced tremendous loneliness, yet he shows the Philippians how to live victoriously right from the pit of that prison.

The next time you feel the wave of loneliness crashing over you, remember that "you do not have a high priest who is unable to sympathize with your weaknesses, but one who has been tempted in every way but was without sin." You can "approach the throne boldly and find mercy and grace to help in your time of need" (Hebrews 4:15-16).

When you need guts to face loneliness, try the following:

*Recognize the lies behind your feeling of loneliness. While our feelings are given to us as a warning sign, they can also lie to us. When we believe that we're not worth being with others, unresolved wounds whisper, "You're a loser, you'll never fit in, no one wants you." God's Word never says any of these things about you, so if you can't find the whispers that you're hearing in God's Word, they're lies.

*Resign from the procrastinator's society. Resist the temptation to do nothing when you feel lonely. Discipline yourself to fill your time by doing something for someone else. Getting ourselves off our own minds and helping others is a great way to alleviate loneliness. When we do, we're motivated to do more the next time we "feel" like doing nothing.

*Resist the urge to have a pity party. Nothing is worse than going to the mirror after a "snot in the carpet" cry and seeing ourselves. We look terrible so we cry harder and the pattern repeats. Been there?

In 2 Timothy, Paul is in prison but he does something amazing. He asks for his coat and his scrolls. Paul was determined to make the best of a bad situation! Paul made the most of his time and as a result, we have a significant part of the New Testament! God can take our darkest days and use them in ways we never imagined. Be like Paul. Refuse to let the enemy of your soul lead you to the party that ends in disaster. Pity parties are for whiners, and you don't have time to attend. You have a destiny.

*Minimize the power of loneliness. Stop rehearsing your hurt. While the Bible commands us to seek wisdom and prayer, no one enjoys being around those who constantly complain. When we complain, the roots of our spiritual tree begin to rot, and we build a wall between ourselves and others. Minimize the power of loneliness by staying in God's Word and meditating on 2 Timothy 4:17: "The Lord stood at my side and gave me strength."

*Consider why you may feel lonely. Do any of the possibilities mentioned above apply to you?

*If a life change has occurred, work on accepting it. God is always willing to open the door to new experiences when we allow Him. Letting go of the old in order to allow the new to move in can be hard. Ask God to help you accept the change and to help you make the transition.

*Challenge yourself to leave the house and get involved in a group or organization that interests you. When you find those who have similar interests, you will find it easier to allow others into your life. Start by going to a function once a month, then once a week. The more you are with other people, the more connections you can make.

*Ask God to bring a new friend into your life. Just as you hope others will be interested in you, show interest in others. Even as I was writing this chapter, someone made the comment to me that I am blessed to have the friends I have. While they are VERY right, I have found it is a two-way street. I strive to be a good friend to others. Show genuine interest in others.

*When establishing a new relationship, remember to go slow. Healthy relationships take time. As you grow new relationships, test the fruit of other's lives. In plain terms, give others time to show you who they really are. Be careful not to overwhelm your new friend with problems or opinions and be a good listener. People will tell you who they are when you listen. If you see "red flags," don't immediately dismiss the relationship, but walk cautiously and watch for repeated patterns that cause concern. While no one is perfect, God longs to place healthy relationships in your life.

*Seize the opportunity to recognize what God may be saying to you when you feel lonely. When I was a teenager (I'm now officially dating myself), Amy Grant sang a song that has lived in my heart for years. I believe the lyrics bear repeating: "I love a lonely day, it makes me think of You. All alone, I can easily find Your love. I love a lonely day, it chases me to You. It clears my heart, let's my very best part shine through, it's You."

At some point, Amy had obviously felt the despair of loneliness and took the time to share her experience of finding God in that place. Instead of asking "Why me, when is it going to change or how long do I have to go through this," ask God, "Will You make Your presence so real to me today that it drowns out any feelings of loneliness?" He will. He "will never leave you or forsake you."

*__Have an outgoing ministry.__ In other words, seek to find someone who is hurting and minister to them. Though we don't "feel" like ministering to others because we're hurting, that's often the time God does the most through us. He uses the pain we're walking through as a conduit of healing to the broken. Hurting people are everywhere and God will lead you to them when you're open to being used as a channel of His love.

Chapter 8

THE GRACE AND GUTS TO MASTER ANGER

Maintaining Control of your Fight

Nothing can make me feel anger like mean people. There are a lot of things we may never be able to afford, but kindness is always free. Since I was a kid, I've always been bothered by mean people. Just ask Billy.

Every night at dusk, my mom would ring a bell for me to come inside for dinner. Once the bell rang, I had five minutes to get home. If I wasn't home in five minutes, I would not be allowed to play outside the next night. I loved playing with the kids in my neighborhood so I always made sure I was on time. I especially loved playing with Angie. She was smaller than all the other kids and since I was tall for my age, our differences made us close friends.

One night at dusk, Angie asked to ride my new bike. Now, this was not just any bike. It was purple with a silver banana seat and silver handlebars with streamers flowing down from the handlebars! I had just gotten this bike for my sixth birthday and I was excited about sharing my new "ride" with my friend.

As I reached out to pass my bike to Angie, Billy came up from behind me and pushed it out of my hands. It hit the ground with a thud. When I picked it up, I saw the long, deep scrape on the rear fender. Unable to understand why a ten-year-old would be so mean, I started to cry. He yanked my bike out of my hands and yelled, "What are you going to do you big crybaby?" Suddenly, I heard my mom ring the bell. I had to get my bike from this bully, and I wasn't going to be late so…I hit him! Just like that, I looked up, saw his brown eyes staring down at me through his wicked smile, and I cocked him right in the nose! He dropped my bike, and I was home in time for dinner.

I didn't tell my mom what happened that night and Billy never told his parents. While I am not a proponent of violence, I've always identified a little with David. That night, I also slew my Goliath with one swing.

Anger. Just the word can stir a memory that makes our heart race. Disrespect shown at work, the neglect of a spouse or harsh words from a friend can send us reeling into hurt, hostility and a desire for revenge. The Greeks defined anger as "the strongest of all passions," and it can be disastrous if we don't learn how to handle it the way Jesus did.

Jesus showed anger when he overturned the tables in the temple. The difference between our anger and His? Our motives are selfish. His motives were holy.

Righteous anger is the godly reaction to sin or injustice. When God demonstrates anger, it is in direct result to sin. When we're His children, we too feel anger towards sin. When we hear of babies being abused and left in a dumpster, we feel angry. God *hates* those things, and we should too.

Sin-filled, or unrighteous anger, is different. It's rooted in fear.

Sinful anger is hard to escape. Turn on the news, and someone is mad. Drive on the freeway, and someone is raging. Go to, dare I say it, church, and someone is hacked off. By nature we are all selfish, so anger leaks into our hearts and out of our mouths more often than we care to admit.

While the world often tells us that we must dig through years of our childhood to address our anger (and in some cases that may be needed), I would like to challenge that belief with a simple example a friend shared with me on YouTube.

The Bob Newhart Show was a TV series back in the late 70's in which Bob Newhart played a psychologist. In a comedy sketch some years later, a "client" was telling Bob Newhart that she was afraid of being buried alive in a box. Every time she tried telling Newhart why she was afraid, he gave her two simple words of advice: "Stop it!" While the skit is hilarious, and you should definitely check it out, I believe there is some truth to Newhart's advice. Could putting our anger aside be as easy as Newhart's advice to his client? Paul seemed to think so.

In Colossians 3:8, Paul reminds us to "**Put aside** all anger, wrath, malice, slander and abusive speech." In other words, just "**stop it!**"

We can find the grace to tame the warhorse of sinful anger when we consider the following:

Analyze your anger honestly. Ask yourself, "Is the anger I'm feeling righteous anger, sinful anger or a mixture of the two? In Genesis 4:6, God asks Cain, "Why are you angry?" We should ask ourselves that same question. When I'm angry, I find there is usually a "sinful" or selfish reason I'm mad.

Control your sinful anger. You may "feel" like you just can't control it, but I'd like to lovingly challenge that thought. While it's hard to become angry and not sin, it is possible. Proverbs 29:11 reminds us that "Fools give full vent to their rage, but the wise bring calm in the end." In other words, the Holy Spirit gives us the ability to practice self-control when we feel angry. We may need to take a step back from the situation, but we will KNOW that the Holy Spirit is in control when we are able to handle our anger in a way that honors God.

Practice the Fruit of the Spirit. We're given the "fruit" of self-control so that we "don't fulfill the desires of the flesh." Fellow drivers in Houston often honk and offer ugly signs out their window when I don't drive to their liking. I implement self-control and refrain from returning their single finger wave.

Memorize key scriptures that relate to anger. What's in our heart will come out of our mouths, especially when we're angry. We can use our tongue like a sword to cut someone's feet out from underneath them, or we can use it like a spoon that feeds healing. Proverbs 12:18 says "There is one who speaks rashly like the thrusts of a sword, but the tongue of the wise brings healing." The reason I wrote and sing the song "Words" for my conferences is because we have all been affected by the angry words of another. "Words have a way of showing love or spewing hate. They can build you up or tear you down. Take you in or throw you out. Words have a way of dashing fires or fanning flames, so be careful what you say, because words have a way." It's always my desperate prayer that I will hide enough of God's Word in my heart so that what leaks out when I'm angry are His words and not my own.

Ask for forgiveness. Even when we feel we have the RIGHT to be angry, we need to repent—to Him and to them if we have handled our anger in any way that's not pleasing to God. Even if *they* were in the wrong, it's not about them. It's about us. It's about our walk and getting to where God wants US to be on our journey. Sin is a blockade, and it separates us from God. Nothing and no one is worth being separated from God or His plan for us.

Pray for those who make you angry. This is a tough one. It's really tough when you still "feel" anger toward the one you're praying for. Keep your prayers focused on YOU. Confess all you feel, and ask the Lord to show you how to handle the situation. He may even lead you to pray *with* that person, so be obedient if He does. While this can feel impossible to your flesh, keep in mind that it's about your heart and the journey you're on with Him. He will deal with them. Just follow what He's telling you to do.

Refuse to retaliate. Nothing can make us feel more "justified" than when we see someone hurt who has hurt us. We may even do a little "fist bump" with God. Be careful. If we've let go of anger and trusted God with the outcome, then no fist bump is needed. Remember, anger doesn't go away on its own. We have to choose to put it aside, and let go of our "right" to retaliate. God can handle the situation MUCH better than we can when we step out of the way and let Him take over.

What if you're on the receiving end of anger? How can we have "guts" when anger is aimed at us? Consider the following:

Listen to the angry person and write down what they're saying. As you write, let the angry person know, "I am writing because I care about what you're saying, and I want to be sure I get everything." As a result, angry people often choose their words differently because they are being held accountable. Warning: If this escalates the person to violence or abuse, put down your pen and paper and walk away. NEVER stay in the presence of an abusive person.

When the angry person finishes talking, ask them if there is anything else they would like to share. Angry people want to feel heard. Listen to the "facts" they share as you keep your heart guarded. The angry person is hurting so they will most likely say something hurtful toward you. Ask God to show you any truth in what they're saying that you may need to address and ignore the rest.

Do NOT respond while you listen. Stay in recorder mode, and write down what is being said.

Take your notes and pray about your response. Set a time to meet back with the person who is angry and let them know you would like to discuss your response at that time. Warning: DO NOT engage if you are feeling angry or upset.

Set a time to meet with the person when you have prayed and can remain calm.

When you meet again, walk away if the angry person escalates. Let them know you are not able to engage in conversation until both of you are calm and can speak to one another in a respectful way.

Take responsibility for any part that may be yours in the discussion. If the angry person points out ways you have been hurtful, ask God to give you the guts to repent for any wrong doing on your part and for the grace to change wrong behaviors.

If violence or abuse is ever present when you're dealing with an angry person, immediately leave their presence and go to a safe place. Always keep your phone charged and with you when dealing with an angry person who has exhibited abusive behavior in the past.

Being slow to anger is a mark of strength and self-control. God is the judge who handles the situations where we've been wronged, so we can let go of our "right" to be angry and retaliate. Proverbs 20:22 gives us this promise: "Do not say, 'I will repay evil;' wait for the Lord and He will save you."

Chapter 9

THE GRACE AND GUTS TO MANAGE DIFFICULT PEOPLE

Winning at Home and in the Workplace

lost my finger this week in a horse accident. Her back foot was caught in her blanket and when I went to unlatch the strap, she lost her balance and fell on me. My middle finger was trapped and when she stood up, she not only broke my finger, she took 80% of the top of my finger with her. Thankfully, I managed to hold my finger on and was able to cut her free before I passed out.

I was rushed to the Emergency Room, and that's when I saw her. The same receptionist that was there the last time I'd come to the ER with my dad. He was having a heart attack, and instead of checking my dad in for immediate assistance, she told my dad to "have a seat" as she sat laughing and talking with her friend on the phone. Now she was on the phone again. I knew what I had to do.

I walked to the desk, looked at her and began screaming. Not just any scream, but an "I'm going to die from pain if you don't sew my finger on now" scream. She slammed the phone down and rushed me into a room. I received immediate help, *and* they saved my finger.

Jane did everything she could do to please her mother-in-law. Belittled and broken, her best efforts failed. One night at dinner, Jane's mother-in-law spewed hurtful and untrue words, claiming Jane was once again in the wrong. This time, Jane practiced healthy boundaries. Jane calmly let her mother-in-law know she would not be able to speak with her when she was shouting and left the room. As a result, Jane's relationship with her mother-in-law improved and a mutual respect was born.

Difficult people seemingly live to make others miserable. When they enter our world, excitement is squelched, memories are marred, and hope is dashed.

If you struggle with difficult people in your life, I have great news. **We do not have to allow other people's misery to infect our lives, nor are we responsible for "fixing" them.** We were never meant to carry the burden of making others happy. Too many times we wear ourselves out trying to do enough, say enough, or give enough only to find it's never enough to satisfy difficult people.

Breaking unhealthy patterns is never easy, but it is possible. I'm a Dr. Pepper nut and love my chocolate more than anything, but if that's all I ever ate, I wouldn't amount to much. You won't either if you continue to place the junk of others in your life and neglect to balance your own. Loving others is a command and that includes the difficult people in our lives. Knowing *how* to love them is key.

In Matthew 10:16, Jesus reminds us "I am sending you out like sheep among wolves. Therefore be as shrewd as snakes and as innocent as doves." Jesus knew there would be those who "play the part" of a loving Christian, but have no "fruit" when closely inspected. Serpents were seen as "crafty" or wise while doves were deemed as one of the clean animals in the Old Testament (Leviticus 14:22). To deal with difficult people, we must have a combination of wisdom (the serpent) and "cleanliness" (the dove).

We can all be difficult at times, so what are the characteristics of a truly difficult person? The Bible gives an excellent description in 2 Timothy 3:1-5. Paul says that difficult people will be "lovers of themselves, lovers of money, boasters, proud, blasphemers, disobedient to parents, unthankful, unholy, unloving, unforgiving, slanderers, without self-control, brutal, headstrong, haughty, lovers of pleasure rather than lovers of God and having a form of godliness, but denying its power." Know anyone who fits that description?

Jesus was always associating with "difficult people," but He always affected them, they never infected Him. While He was changing their lives, Jesus never allowed anyone to change Him.

You may recognize some of the behaviors Paul describes in 2 Timothy in your home, workplace, or, even in yourself. Does that mean you are a difficult person? While all of us can be demanding and selfish at times, difficult people *maintain* a pattern of bad behavior. Difficult people feel no remorse for their bad behavior. They may *say* they're sorry for what they have done, but they are usually just sorry they got caught. They are rarely able to feel true remorse for hurting another. There is one person who usually matters to a difficult person: themselves. Others matter when they can serve the difficult person in some capacity. Difficult people are like dying trees. When a tree is rotten at the root, the fruit begins to die. Difficult people can put on a show for a while, but eventually, their true colors come to light. Most difficult people fall into one of the following categories:

*The Controller—The controller wants to be in charge—of everything. They are masters at micro-managing and are ready, willing, and able to pinpoint flaws in the lives of others while refusing to acknowledge any flaws of their own.

*The Blamer—It's never their fault and the responsibility always lies with others. They are masters at convincing themselves and everyone else that they are not to blame for their choices.

*The Bully—Power is the food they need to survive and their objective is to wear others down so that they are in control.

*The Nay-Sayers—They rarely have anything positive to say and tend to be whiners that zap the energy from ideas as quickly as they are born. They believe the worst about most things—even people they claim to love.

The Prideful—They are arrogant and rarely think they're wrong. They are quick to judge, to offer their opinions, and are rude to others who they view as subservient. Their goal is to appear superior and right in all situations.

The Victim—They have not been truly victimized, but are needy and will tell you how they have been done wrong as long as you will listen. Their goal is to keep all of the attention focused on them.

The Abuser—They take out their own experiences of past hurts and trauma by being cruel and dangerous to those they claim to "care for" the most. Their abuse can be sexual, verbal, physical, mental, emotional, spiritual or a combination of all.

The Addict—The addict habitually surrenders to a substance or negative behavior pattern, destroying their life and the lives of those around them.

The Gossip—The gossip gains power from retrieving information that others may not know. They are usually vicious with their words and have no regard for the feelings or reputation of another person.

"Difficult people" are everywhere, so how do we respond with grace and guts when we cross their path?

THE GUTS TO CONQUER "DIFFICULT PEOPLE" AT WORK:

It doesn't take long to spot a condescending co-worker. They sneer when you make a suggestion or avoid acknowledging you altogether. They act like they know everything and you know nothing.

Co-workers who display such behavior are desperately insecure. While that doesn't remove the pain they inflict, it gives us the grace to emulate Jesus.

God may ask you to say nothing to your co-worker. While extremely hard, we learn self-control and submission to what God requires. If He calls you to action, try the following:

Respond in a quiet, controlled manner. Maintaining your cool with a belittling co-worker can be tough, but responding calmly is key. You might say, "I understand you don't like the way I filed the paperwork today. I'm ready to hear you calmly state the ways you'd like for me to improve. I have a pen and a piece of paper so that I get all of your concerns in writing. I want to be sure that both of us are happy with my performance moving forward."

Take the emotion out of your reaction. If the conversation turns hurtful or abusive, let your co-worker know you are unable to listen until they can talk with you respectfully and then walk away. While God does require us to love others, He has never required us to be doormats.

- **Put distance between you and your difficult co-worker**. Take your breaks outside or at a park. If that's not possible, sit at your desk, put on your headphones and listen to worship music as you read God's Word. Deciding how you will spend any free time at work will help you feel more in control of your day.

- **If your difficult co-worker becomes abusive, alert their superiors.** Others in the company are probably experiencing difficulties but are too afraid to say anything. When reporting abusive behavior, keep your report factual. Avoid emotion and personal commentary. Whatever you report will most likely go on record.

- **Surround yourself with co-workers who support you.** Find kind, fun and energetic people who breathe life into your difficult workplace. If there is no one at work who fits this description, find someone outside of work who speaks hope to your heart and can pray for you while on the job.

While God may nudge you to change jobs, jumping from job to job can be more disabling than a difficult co-worker. If you're tempted to leave your job, seek God before you do. He may be allowing you to pass through the fire of a "difficult" co-worker before promoting you, so stay faithful and watch closely for new doors He may be opening.

THE GUTS TO FACE "DIFFICULT PEOPLE" IN OUR FAMILY:

Audra and Lisa disagreed about selling their mom's home after she died. Lisa needed the money and wanted to sell the house, while Audra refused to put the house on the market. Lisa became angry toward Audra and, eventually, the closeness and communication they once enjoyed disintegrated.

There are few things that add stress to our lives like fighting with family members. Difficult family members may never change, but we can.

When family members are difficult:

***Remember your difficult family member is created and loved by God**. Remember that you are created and loved by God as well. Don't overlook your value when dealing with difficult family.

***Refuse disrespect.** Lovingly remind your family member that you will not tolerate hurtful behavior. This may be done physically by removing yourself from their presence, or you may need to verbalize your boundary. For example, "John, when you yell at me I am not able to stay in the same room. I am happy to talk with you when you are calm." You may have to repeat this numerous times and sadly, some may never get it until you set additional boundaries.

***Establish consequences**. For example: "I've talked with you about this, and it doesn't seem that you're hearing what I'm saying. As a result, I won't be able to interact with you until (name their bad behavior) changes." This is a hard one, but keep in mind that consequences often help heal a relationship.

***Don't go it alone.** If the boundaries you set are not respected, take someone with you who can stay neutral in the situation. If you lack support, one of two things may be happening: 1) you are contributing to the problem in some way and need to ask others how that may be happening, or 2) you are surrounded by people who have chosen to live outside of truth and refuse to acknowledge the problem.

Sadly, there are family members who will support one another no matter how dysfunctional the behavior. If you are the only one in the family who stands for truth, find another person who is emotionally healthy and will help keep you grounded in God's truth. If you are the only healthy family member, you are not the "dodo" lost in the forest. Dysfunctional people believe their behavior is normal and when you are surrounded by dysfunction, it is a lonely and confusing place. Don't be afraid to stand your ground. When you set healthy boundaries, you can impact generations.

THE GUTS TO CONFRONT THOSE WHO IGNORE US:

Difficult people intentionally "stonewall" by withdrawing emotionally and using silence as punishment.

If multiple attempts have been made to make peace with those who ignore you, consider the following:

1. **Your worth and value comes from God alone**. When others intentionally ignore us, they are sending the message that we don't exist. God says we are "fearfully and wonderfully made," and He is very displeased with those who intentionally denigrate His creation. We have to stop wearing ourselves out seeking approval from those who don't even acknowledge that we exist. Too many times we think if we just do one more thing, it might be exactly what we need to do to receive the attention we desire. The truth is that if God wants for someone to acknowledge and receive us, He will make a way. We don't have to force it. Take the pressure off yourself today and let God bring you before those He has destined for your life.

2. **Remind yourself that it's not about you**. When difficult people refuse to reconcile after our purest

attempts at peace, we have done what God asks us to do. While we may still have to be in a relationship with our difficult person, we can walk in peace when we "keep our side of the street clean" by pursuing peace.

3. **Understand the logic behind the silent treatment**. Those who practice the silent treatment as a means of control like to prey on our fears. They try to gain control by withholding the love or approval we desire. Often, we lose sight of truth and become desperate for acceptance. As a result, we may do "whatever" it takes to receive the love and attention we desire. This is a snare of the enemy. DO NOT take the bait. You are never alone and will always have someone who loves and supports you. God Almighty is there for you and He is able to send whoever and whatever you need. HE is your provider. HE is your sustainer. HE is your rock. Run to Him and get all you need from Him.

4. **Don't believe the lies**. When a difficult person uses silence to control, it is known as abuse. Abusive people tell others it is their fault they are receiving abuse, but we are never responsible for another's abusive behavior.

5. **Don't respond to hurtful behavior**. This is one of the hardest things we will do with difficult people. We're repeatedly told in God's Word to "love" the way that Jesus did. When He was on the cross, Jesus didn't speak a word to those who were killing Him. How can we respond in love to those who are hurting us? Ignore their behavior. When we fight, cry, beg or plead for another's attention, we are dishonoring God. God did

not say, "I guess that will do" when He created you. He created you in His own image. When others mistreat you, they are mistreating the Holy Spirit in you.

6. **Do not reward the silent treatment**. Too many times we try harder when we need to back off. The next time your difficult person implements the silent treatment, refuse to acknowledge it. When a child throws himself on the ground in a temperamental rage because they want a toy, do you give it to them? Of course not! You walk away and refuse to reward bad behavior. The same applies to those who ignore us. Instead of giving them the control they want by crying, texting, demanding, or pouting, move on with what God has purposed for your day and leave them in His hands. That's a good place for the difficult people in our lives.

As you deal with difficult people, it's important to surround yourself with those who value you. Difficult people erode our sense of self and will go to great lengths to have us believe the worst about ourselves. Surround yourself with those who remind you of the beautiful person you were created to be. If you have difficulty believing truth because you've heard so many lies, read the Psalms and ask God to give you a fresh revelation of His love for you. He loves you with an everlasting love. Your worth and value are found only in Him.

Chapter 10

THE GRACE AND GUTS TO BATTLE DEPRESSION

Throwing Your Best Hit When You Feel Like Throwing in the Towel

Depression transcends sadness and removes our ability to think clearly. It makes us sleep more, eat less or eat everything in sight. According to research, one in every eight women will experience clinical depression during their lifetime (mentalhealthamerica.net). Even more will experience symptoms that are not formally diagnosed. While depression is treatable, many suffer in silence due to the shame, stigma, and "un-Christian-like" labels placed on them. How could a

"Christian" woman be depressed after all? Isn't the "joy of the Lord" her strength?

When we are depressed we often suffer alone, cry ourselves to sleep, or remain hidden from others because we feel misunderstood, abandoned or ashamed. Jesus understands, and He came to set us free from bondage, including the labels and humiliation associated with depression.

Depression is not a moral issue, bad mood, or a reflection of our character. Depression is caused by a chemical imbalance in the brain. It takes great courage and strength to fight this debilitating illness and those who fight depression are some of the strongest and most lovely people I know. While aware of their struggle, they refuse defeat. Doctors' visits, counseling, and prayer are usually a part of their recovery, and for some, prescribed medication. They prayerfully consider the need for medication and refuse to live in shame if it's needed. When depression raises its ugly head, they raise their gloves to fight.

Depression sneaks in like an unwelcomed robber. It steals our energy, appetite, sleep, and hope. When depression strikes, you may notice:

- Disturbed sleep patterns: sleeping all the time, not at all or sporadically throughout the night
- A drastic increase or decrease in appetite
- A loss of interest in things you used to enjoy
- Crying easily, frequently, or for no apparent reason
- An overwhelming feeling of sadness or the inability to be happy

- Unusual irritability
- Difficulty focusing on the "big picture" because little details are overwhelming
- Inability to enjoy intimacy with your spouse
- Angry outbursts due to feelings of helplessness
- Difficulty concentrating or making decisions; easily distracted
- Sluggish, slowed movement; no longer exercise, fatigued
- Feelings of worthlessness, guilt, or focus on past failures
- Thoughts of ending your life

Elijah was acquainted with depression. In I Kings 19, Elijah goes from the hilltop of victory to a valley of despair when Jezebel threatens to kill him. In one day, this mighty man of God transitions from confident warrior to depressed recluse. It's possible for spiritual people to be depressed too!

Elijah begs God to take his life before falling asleep under a juniper tree. An angel awakens Elijah and tells him to eat. Notice that the angel addresses Elijah's physical needs first. We must be physically nurtured or we feel "off." That's why people who have physical imbalances in their brain as a result of depression may not need more prayer, they may need a doctor. When we're hungry, we don't need a Bible study, we need a bowl of dumplings! If someone is depressed, we must consider the possibility that there is a physical condition affecting their emotional state.

The second time the angel comes to Elijah, he receives enough food to last forty days and forty nights. THAT is supernatural, and THAT is how God works. When we pray an honest prayer of desperation for God, He shows up in supernatural ways. God sustains Elijah because He knows what he will need to face his future. He knows what you need, too.

Elijah is also instructed to go to the mountain of God because he isn't doing well on his own. When Elijah talked to himself, he was suicidal. When he talked to God, he was transformed. God knew that Elijah needed the truth of His presence, not the lies he was hearing between his ears. When we feel depressed, we must get to God's presence. He doesn't ask us to come to Him when we "feel" like it. He commands it because He knows we can get what we need. We may go crying, screaming, or barely able to whisper, but when we lay before God in our most vulnerable state, powerful things happen.

When Elijah gets to the mountain, there is a great wind, earthquake and fire, but God was not in any of those. He was in the still, soft breeze. The lesson? The presence of God and the help that we need may show up in unexpected ways. The loud demonstrations of nature did not contain God's spirit. It was the quiet breeze; a still small voice. Too many times we're looking for the "wow" or what we "think" God should do in our situation when He is doing the unexpected.

God also reminds Elijah that there are 7,000 others who believe as he does. One of the reasons we need to be active in the body of Christ is because we need the support of others. Fellow believers don't allow us to be defeated by depression, but lift us out of depression with love and truth. There have been times in my life that I needed help fighting the lies in my head.

I needed friends who would "speak the truth" in love and when they did, my perspective became clearer. Find those who will speak the truth of God's Word to you when you are depressed. Friends like that are invaluable.

Depression that is left untreated can lead to despair. When despair is untreated, it leads to hopelessness. When we apply God's Word to conquer hopelessness, we find grace and guts to battle depression courageously.

THE GUTS TO CONQUER HOPELESSNESS:

A little bird was flying south for the winter. As he flew through the cold, his wings began to freeze and eventually he couldn't fly. He fell into a pasture where a herd of cows were grazing. One cow walked by and dropped manure on him. He was very angry until he realized that the warm manure made him feel good and helped thaw his wings. He got so happy that he began to sing. A cat that was walking through the pasture heard the bird singing and began to dig through the pile of manure. When he found the bird, he ate him.

While this is not a true story, there's a valuable lesson to be learned. Manure *can* yield positive results as long as we are aware that the enemy may come digging.

The enemy loves to find us in the manure. He came to "steal, kill and destroy" and loves to kick us when we're down. Thoughts like "I'm worthless, it will never get better or I'll never be ok" are straight from Satan's doorstep. His goal is to make us crater under pressure, lose hope, and feel we can't move on. If we quit, we're no longer effective. Satan knows the dangerous dent you can hurl against the kingdom of darkness when you have hope. He also knows how ineffective you will be for the Kingdom of God if you're hopeless.

Hope is found throughout God's Word. The next time you encounter hopelessness, consider the following:

1. **Apply Psalm 46:10**. "Be still and know that I am God." When we face a situation that seems too much to bear, God already knows the next move. The hardest part? Being still. We become so used to "doing something," it can feel impossible to sit still and wait on God when we need answers NOW! I have learned that God NEVER works on my timetable. He's never late, and He's never early (although I sure wish He would be sometimes). He wants us to "know" that He is God. When we "know" something, we live with hope. When we "know" God, we develop confidence in the One who gives us hope. You can live with great confidence in Jesus today because He "knows" you. He knows right where you are, how long you've been there, and how to get you through. The best part? He will! It may not be on your timetable, but hold on, He's coming!

2. **Allow God to heal you.** When we feel hopeless, we can believe that even God Himself has given up on us. This is a lie. Each time your emotions scream the lies of hopelessness, recite Psalm 42:11: "Why, my soul, are you downcast? Why so disturbed within me? Put your hope in God for I will yet praise Him, my Savior and my God." Repeat this over and over. Say it out loud. The more your mind hears the truth, the sooner your

perspective changes. God wants to heal you. Believe it and let Him.

3. **Don't put a time limit on yourself or God.** Sometimes, we feel so hopeless for so long that we want to give up. I've found that God allows this in my own life when He's ready to move supernaturally. There's no way the situation will change unless He does something. When it does change, I never doubt who intervened. When we wait on God, He promises to renew our strength according to Isaiah 40:31. If waiting is not your strength, I get that, but He *will* bring strength in the waiting. Once you find that strength, begin to look for ways that God is working in your situation and write them down. Then, thank Him.

4. **Believe there is more beyond what you've experienced or seen.** How many times have you started the day feeling hopeless about a situation, only to find that you have hope by nightfall? When we are actively waiting with hope for God to move, He does. He will never fail us. It may not look like we thought it would, but He will move. His will is the best place to be, so rest. The responsibility is on His shoulders and He knows how to put every piece in place.

5. **Squelch the urge to quit.** Too many times we quit when we are right on the verge of a breakthrough. Refuse to allow anything to move you unless God says move. We all have something trying to move us out of the will of God. When we feel like quitting, we have to stand and let our obstacle know "You will not

move me!" Say it out loud! Even if you have to say it 100 times a day. This not only reminds the enemy that you are here for the long-haul, it reminds you, too. Everything coming against you is trying to move you. Fight and let that "thing" know that you will go all the way with God because He's the One you're trusting. Stay on the Potter's Wheel and let Him finish the beautiful masterpiece that He is completing in you.

After losing my mom to cancer, I have realized that I will NEVER be the same. I just have a "new normal." She was my best friend, my secretary, my traveling buddy and the one who could make me laugh like no one else. There are no words to describe the hole that was left in my heart when she died. What God has shown me, however, is that I still have a purpose and He needs me to fulfill it.

If you are facing depression due to a loss, God is a redeeming God and He will help you beat depression and move forward as you:

1. **Face the loss in a healthy way.** Acknowledge that the loss has happened and the pain is real. Allow yourself to cry or deal with your emotions in productive ways. Avoid wallowing in self-pity or participating in things that are harmful. For many of us, crying comes naturally, but some of us have a difficult time releasing our emotions. Find a healthy outlet for your pain. Pray, talk to Christian friends or a counselor who can guide you through God's Word. You may also want

to do something physical like screaming at the top of your lungs in a solitary place. I've done it and it feels great! It was just God and I, and while I knew there was no need to shout, I knew He understood my pain. Whether you go for a run or complete a project you've been wanting to finish, do something that helps you productively press on.

2. **Find others who understand loss**. There are numerous support groups that focus on grief and loss. Find a supportive group of friends or an individual who will help carry you as you grieve. A trained counselor, someone who has experienced loss, a grief support or a Bible Study class where others have experienced loss are all great networks to help you heal.

3. **Release guilt**. The day before mom died, I was wiping her lips because they were dry. I didn't have a washcloth so I used a paper towel. As I wiped she said, "Ouch! That's rough." What may seem a small infraction to you was huge in my world. For years I had worked tirelessly to care for her with excellence and that was one of the last times she spoke. I carried guilt for months over using that paper towel instead of a washcloth.

When we are in duress, we often deal with things differently. If your behavior was inappropriate at the time of your loss or you feel guilt for something you did unintentionally, tell God, and let it go. When we focus on what we "wish" we would have said or done, we get stuck. Release your guilt, knowing you were doing the best you could at the time. Ask Him to take away your pain and redeem your negative experience with something positive. He *is* a redeeming God. The last time my mom ever spoke, she took my hand and told me she was giving me a gift. I've often wondered if it was her sweet way of giving me a soft washcloth!

4. **Find productive activities to help you move forward as you grieve.** Nothing says you must be "totally healed" of grief before you move forward. Begin to live as normal as possible as you commit to working through your loss. Take baby steps if necessary. Praise God that you got out of bed and took a shower. The next day, praise Him that you got out of bed, took a shower and made your bed. Keep moving forward as God performs His healing work in your heart.

5. **Surround yourself with those who will help you ease back into your social roles.** While it may feel awkward that neither you nor your friends know how to approach your loss, don't hibernate. It may take a few months to feel like getting back into normal activities, but the support of those who love you is crucial. Talk with a friend on the phone or go have dinner together, but get around those who care about you and let God bring the confidence you need to ease back into larger groups.

6. **Be patient with yourself.** Experiencing grief is one thing, but faking happiness is another. Be genuine in your relationships and with yourself. Each day, journal one thing that you feel has been a gradual improvement in your life. When you feel stuck, review

your journal and celebrate the days that you did the dishes when you didn't feel like it or went to work when you wanted to sleep. That is a positive step on your road to healing.

7. **Pray daily**. Release every emotion that you are experiencing to God and continue to ask Him for comfort and healing as you cry out to Him. When you cry out, remember that He can handle your anger, pain, questions, and brokenness. He promises healing in I Peter 5:10: "After your season of suffering, God in all His grace will restore, confirm, strengthen and establish you." THAT is His promise just for *you*, and He is faithful to complete it.

Chapter 11

THE GRACE AND GUTS TO BEAT UNCERTAINTY

Winning over Worry in Every Stage of Life

"Life seldom turns out the way you plan it." I don't know about you, but this line from my song "Keep Pressing On" rings very true in my own life. When I think back to the way I thought my life would be as I was growing up, some things have certainly come to pass. I always wanted to be a teacher and I was in the education field for fourteen years as a teacher and counselor. I also wanted to sing professionally and minister to crowds. God exceeded my expectations by allowing me to speak, have a television show and many other avenues for ministry. I always wanted to be a wife and mom, and I am both today. While God has allowed many of my dreams to transpire, the journey I took to get to my dreams is another story. Life has a way of taking us on a crazy ride and when we don't know where the ride will end, it can be scary.

I am a huge fan of Hallmark movies. I love the way they make me feel and even more, I love that I know how they are going to end. They always have a twist, but always end the same. Love conquers all, there is a lot of clapping and cheering, and everyone smiles as they go back to their perfectly decorated homes. I'd like to live in that kind of certainty, wouldn't you?

There is assurance when we know how things will end. When we don't, it can set us into a tailspin of fear and uncertainty. We have no idea how we will face the world when our kids leave home. We don't know how we will pay next month's bills when we lose our job. We long to be married, but can't find the right one. A loved one dies, and we don't know how we can go on without them.

Life takes us through different seasons. With change comes uncertainty, fear, and unrest because it's not a Hallmark movie we're living. It's real life. Our dreams get shattered, someone goes away who promised to stay, or our kids turn out to be nothing like we raised them to be. We have no idea how to change what's happening, and the fear of how it may all turn out knocks us to our knees!

When uncertainty comes knocking, fear screams that the worst will happen. Faith reminds us that the Creator of the Universe is still sitting on His throne. One night when I was lighting our gas grill, I was reminded that God is always in control and can certainly save us from the worst, even when we create it.

Preparing to make steaks, I turned on all four burners of the grill and walked away for 30 minutes. When I returned, the lid of the grill was cold. Without raising the lid, I turned all the burners off and reignited the first burner. As I did, a flame exploded from underneath the lid of the grill and engulfed me in flames. The gas had been on, but the burners had not.

My husband and dad both heard the explosion and came running into the backyard to find me trying to extinguish the fire on top of my head! I just knew that my face had melted off! Amazingly, the only hair lost was the end of my ponytail and my bangs. Since I had to take pictures the next day, I found a good stylist and no one knew the difference. What could have been a life-altering experience turned out to be a simple inconvenience because God protected me. One friend said, "I'm glad you didn't look like what you had been through when you took your pictures." Aren't you glad we don't have to look like the "fires" we've been through?

Maybe you have had an "explosion" in your life and you're facing uncertainty. An unexpected medical diagnosis has invaded your life or a dream that seemed certain has ended in disappointment. The "fires" of uncertainty have left you feeling aimless and lost. It's often in the uncertainty that we experience the greatest gift. The opportunity to "try on" our faith.

There are simply going to be times that we don't know how the money will be there or how the relationship will turn out. Plans are going to fall through, circumstances will change and people will disappoint us. Jesus experienced it, and we will too.

One of the most powerful reminders God sends for us in times of uncertainty is found in Romans 8:26: "In the same way, the Spirit helps us in our weakness for we DO NOT KNOW what we ought to pray for, but the Spirit Himself intercedes for us through wordless groans." Notice the words "DO NOT KNOW." The Spirit Himself knew we would face uncertainty and WOULD NOT KNOW what to pray. Uncertainty is no surprise to God. The unknown was part of His plan.

If you stop to think about it, we're all going in a direction that we've never been before. You have never been your age. You have never lived this moment. You're the parent of a toddler once. If you rear another one, it's still uncertain because they're nothing like the first one you reared. The more we do things, the more we learn how much we really don't know. Experience teaches us to respect what we're up against.

Life is full of uncertainty simply because we're all doing things for the first time and we don't know what we're doing. James 1:5 reminds us that when we lack wisdom, we "should ask God, who gives generously to all without finding fault… and it will be given to you." God does not snub His nose to us when we feel uncertain. He warmly welcomes our uncertainty and guides us through our "firsts."

Only fools believe they know everything. Wisdom admits, "I don't know," and is open to learning. The only time we usually "think" we know everything is when we've never done it. For example, I'm an expert football coach from my living room, but put me on the field and it would be disastrous! I've never done it. The beginning of wisdom is learning what you don't know.

When I travel to a new place, it's stressful because it's uncertain. I've never been there before so I usually turn the radio off and listen for direction from my GPS (which I've programmed to speak in a lovely male British accent).

I love to shop because part of the adventure is the uncertainty. Whether online or in the mall, I love to look at all the possibilities that are available. In all my years of shopping, I've never thought, "I'm probably not going to find anything anyway." I always begin my shopping experience with expectation. Sometimes I find what I'm looking for, and sometimes I don't. Sometimes, I get more than what I expected. The way God works in our uncertainty is similar. Sometimes we find that He does what we were expecting and sometimes He doesn't. Sometimes, He exceeds our expectations. One thing is certain—He will always work in our uncertainty when we're trusting Him.

Have you noticed that we resolve most of our issues in the middle of uncertainty? When you see an older couple holding hands in the mall, there's a reason they're not arguing about anything. They worked it out in the middle. The middle is where we stay on the Potter's wheel and see things through when it's toughest.

Are you focused on the good things that God can do in the middle of your situation instead of focusing on the negative? Being laid off from your job could be the path to finding your dream job. Your health scare could be the thing that refocuses your priorities. Rejection in a relationship could be what leads to finding the right person for your life. God has an amazing way of leading us to certainty when we trust Him in our most uncertain times.

Maybe you don't see how God *could* bring anything good from your circumstances. If not, put your "faith glasses" on. It's easy to say we trust God until we're in a place where we can't see His hand. A friend of mine wrote a great lyric years ago that bears repeating: "When you can't trace His hand, trust His heart." Living in the unknown is the best chance we'll get to see that our God is faithful. It's one thing to say we have faith. It's another to watch it come to life when we see no way through.

If you need the guts to regain your focus during uncertain times, take the following into consideration:

1. **Take One Step at a Time**. While this may be obvious, it can be really hard to do.

2. **Get Organized**. Uncertainty can leave us spinning in circles. As a result, we become disoriented, disorganized and frustrated. Make a daily plan and follow it to keep what you DO have control over moving in an organized and purposeful direction.

3. **Avoid looking too far into the future**. When we begin looking in the distance, we often begin to imagine things that may or may not happen, and the "what if's" become overwhelming. Keep your focus on what God is doing in the present, and thank Him as you take one step at a time.

4. **Refuse the lies.** When we're insecure, uncertainty lies. "God will never help you through this one. It's over. You're doomed. It's going to be the worst." Take

authority over insecurity, and refuse to believe any of those lies.

5. **Focus on previous success.** Focus on the previous times in your life that God has come through for you. One of the greatest lies Satan whispers is "God may have come through for you before, but *this* time, He won't." God is faithful, Satan is always a liar, and God WILL come through for you again.

6. **Enter into Worship.** Uncertainty creates pressure, and worship alleviates pressure. Have you noticed that you can't truly worship and worry at the same time? As Stormie Omartian said so eloquently, "Praise is the prayer that changes everything."

7. **Surrender.** LET GO! Tell Him you don't know so He can show you what *He* does know.

8. **Release guilt.** Guilt makes us feel anxious and unworthy to receive God's help because we know who we "really" are. The good news is from God's promise in Romans 8:1: "There is therefore now no condemnation to those who are in Christ Jesus." Guilt is gone and help has arrived.

There is no shame in uncertainty because we weren't designed to know everything. That's why we need a Savior. He's all-knowing, all-powerful and is certainly moving even when we feel like He isn't. We can turn down the noise of fear and turn up the trust because "God is not a man that He should lie, nor a son of man that He should repent; has He said and will He not do it? Or has He spoken, and will He not make it good?"

This promise from Numbers 23:19 is a solemn vow that we can cling to during times of uncertainty. While life is a string of uncertainty, we have a tightrope of faith.

Chapter 12

THE GRACE AND GUTS TO CHAMPION OUR PURPOSE

Becoming a Heavyweight Champion with God as Your Coach

I need to tell you a secret. This book was going to contain eleven chapters until I did a survey on Facebook. I felt God may have one more chapter I needed to write, so I posted this question to my Facebook friends: "In what area have you seen women struggle the most?" One answer was unanimous. Women want to know how to find purpose for their lives.

We know that the overall purpose for each of our lives as Christians is found in Matthew 28:16-20. "The Great

Commission" commands us to GO and MAKE DISCIPLES. Whatever we do with our time, talent or titles, our focus is to be eternal. Souls are all that last for eternity and our purpose is to lead them to Jesus.

If it's that simple, why are so many of us living with no clue of what to do with our lives? Finding the answer may be easier than you think.

First, I want to assure you that God really does have a specific plan just for you. No matter what season of life you're in, if you're still breathing, you have a purpose. Too many times I hear, "I'm too old, too young, too uneducated or I have no talent." Can't you just hear the disciples saying the same things? They were fishermen and tax collectors who were quite comfortable doing what they had to do to make ends meet. When Jesus called the disciples to be His followers, He met them right where they were and chose to use them in spite of where they had been. He was concerned with only one thing— their heart. Jesus never asked them, "How talented are you? How much money do you have? How old are you? Are you insecure?" As He called them, He simply said, "Follow Me." Their answer determined their destiny.

How has your answer affected your destiny? Some people who have spoken to me about their purpose say they know what it is, but they're not doing it. They're afraid of being rejected, they're scared of what others think, or believe they're not good enough. Notice who it's all about? The student, not the Teacher. One brings peace; the other brings fear.

Matthew 8:24 illustrates a beautiful contrast between peace and fear. Jesus and the disciples are out on the lake in a boat.

"Suddenly a furious storm came up on the lake, so that the waves swept over the boat. But Jesus was sleeping." Jesus was sleeping? Have you BEEN in a boat when it's being tossed in a storm? I have, and it's one of the most out-of-control feelings I've ever experienced!

The next verse tells us that "The disciples went and woke him, saying, 'Lord, save us! We're going to drown!'" Can you almost feel yourself in that boat right now? Picture it. You've got your bright pink raincoat on (ok, choose your color) with matching rain boots, of course, and you had planned to ride casually across the lake with Jesus to do ministry. Suddenly, this storm comes out of nowhere, and you forget everything you've learned about Jesus because you're freaking out! While we know how this story ends, the disciples did not. Jesus reminds the disciples that He is in control and rebukes them by saying, "You of little faith, why are you so afraid?" Jesus got up, rebuked the wind and waves and calmed everything, including the disciples. The disciples received a powerful lesson that day—sometimes Jesus is quiet during the storm.

Do you remember taking a quiz when you were in school? The teacher taught a lot before the test, but the day of the quiz, she sat at her desk silently or even left the room at times. She was no longer teaching. She was waiting to see how much we'd learned during the lessons we'd been taught.

God is waiting patiently for some of us to reveal how much we've learned from His instructions in our life. He's grown silent because we're taking the test.

For years, I asked God about the possibility of doing television. For years, I heard nothing. When God finally opened the door for me to do television, I literally laughed out loud! I have absolutely no formal training for being in front of a camera and thought surely He would have introduced me to TV in a different way. I expected that I would be more experienced, educated and formally trained before He put me in front of a camera. As I began to present my case before God, all I kept hearing Him say was "trust Me."

Slowly, ideas for the show began to unravel. We did pilot shows, and I hired people to help film. We laugh today because those shows were shot with the hottest lights ever made. I didn't know to get halogen lights at the time, so we had to take multiple breaks because the lights kept blowing a fuse when we were taping. I didn't know what I was doing, but God's plan began taking shape in spite of me.

The day someone purchased two TV cameras for our ministry, I was no longer laughing. I was on my face thanking God that He could take such incompetence, inexperience and lack of confidence and use me anyway.

God allows us to walk through experiences so we can minister to others and fulfill His purpose for our life. We are the ones that make it complicated. Too many times we get our minds fixed on our gifts and talents, or lack thereof, and miss the opportunity to fulfill our purpose as a result of the tests we have taken.

In Matthew 14, Jesus commands Peter to come to Him by walking on the water. Peter walks confidently because He has learned from experience that when this teacher asks something of His student, He helps them pass the test. Peter steps out of the boat fully confident—until he focuses on the waves crashing around him and begins to sink. Peter forgot who called him to get out of the boat.

Could it be that you can't find your purpose today because fear and doubt have caused you to forget *who* called you out of the boat?

Paul must have been thinking of failure in Philippians 3:13-14. After all, he had certainly had his share. You think you're unqualified to serve God with your purpose? This guy murdered Christians before his conversion to Jesus!

Paul's words in verse 13 serve as a powerful reminder when we begin to feel we've failed in our purpose. He writes, "Forgetting what lies behind and reaching forward to what lies ahead, I press on toward the goal for the prize of the upward call of God in Christ Jesus." There's that word—call. It's used and misused at times, but our call is our purpose. Paul gives a strong warning to those who want to excel in their purpose: *Stop looking back!*

We can evaluate where and how we failed in order to learn and grow, however, the past is never to be our focus. When we do look at our past, there are a couple of things to consider:

1. **If we have failed multiple times at trying something we believed to be our calling, we may be serving outside of our gift.** Romans 12:3 tells us "not to think more highly of ourselves than we should think." We need to be sure that the gifts and talents God has placed in us are in line with what we are trying to accomplish. For example, you will not see me trying to fix the electric box in someone's

home when it goes out because I would blow their house apart!

2. **If you have had multiple failed attempts at what you believe to be your calling, you may be trying to do things your own way.** How do we know God's way? We read His Word, pray and we walk through open doors. When God presents your purpose to you, He's going to open doors to fulfill it. God does not play some cruel joke on us by making us beg for ways to use our gifts and talents. He created us to bring Him glory through our purpose!

3. **When we've had failed attempts at what we believe to be our calling, we may need to put ourselves on the altar and tell God He can direct us any way He desires.** After all, He created us. We were not born to find our purpose. We were born WITH our purpose. When we get a computer from the store, we don't have to download all of the information the computer needs. The information is already there! The same goes for your purpose. God has placed all you need in you. The question is not *can* you but *will* you allow God to work through you however He chooses?

Oftentimes we're willing for God to use us, but doubt that He will. We try something once, and if we fail, we immediately assume we must not be "enough" for our calling. We forget that He's stamped the symbol of His Son on us. That symbol comes with a high price. It also comes with an amazing guarantee.

My car has a symbol on it. That symbol represents the manufacturer's reputation. My car also comes with a manual that tells me everything my car can do. How do they know? Because they have tested and re-tested my car so they can guarantee it can perform all the actions it is designed to do.

God is your manufacturer and He has placed His symbol on your life because, just like my car, the Manufacturer knows your design. Although I don't believe I have *ever* read an entire manual for *anything* I own, I did learn that my car will do 37 things I didn't know it could do because I read the back of the manual.

My point? I paid a lot of money for a car to not utilize all it has to offer. The same goes with us! Jesus paid the highest price for us not to utilize all of the gifts and talents God has given us.

I also noticed that the last two pages of any manual always includes two words—warranty and guarantee. Warranty means that the company will pay for all shipping, repairs and parts at no charge to the customer. The company offers that because they want to keep their reputation and name in good standing.

So many times we think that God is going to do or not do something because of our gifts or lack thereof. In reality, *it's not about us*. It's about the symbol we are wearing—HIS name. When God created you, He downloaded EVERYTHING you need to fulfill the call and purpose He has for your life.

So how do you identify the call? Learn how you are wired.

I am a mouth in the body of Christ. They used to put me in the corner for talking too much in school. Now, they're paying me to talk. Communication is one of my strengths, and I have been made keenly aware of my gift my entire life. It didn't take me long to figure out that I am not a "cook" in the body of Christ. I tried to cook for the sick people of the church once, and they were worse when I left! Too many times we are running around trying to do things that God never called us to do, and we're miserable because of it.

So how do we "stay in our lane" when it comes to our purpose? Some of us can't even figure out where the road is much less how to get into our lane. We've tried so many things, and we just can't figure out our purpose. How do we find it? The following are a few things I have learned about finding purpose and I pray they can be used as the map that helps you find your lane today.

1. **Listen to your dissatisfaction**. God takes delight in using us in areas we enjoy. It won't be "easy," but there will be a peace when we're serving in the place God has called us to serve. When we're unhappy or lose our peace for an extended period of time in our area of service, it may be that God is leading us into another lane. Don't let that scare you; embrace it. Change is good! I have learned that when I am unhappy or lose my peace for an extended period of time in some area of service, it's because God's anointing is no longer on me to do that thing. It doesn't mean He's done with me. It means He's moving, and I need to move with Him.

    When we try to "hold on" in an area where God is saying, "let go," we're trying to walk in an anointing that is no longer ours. Stay under the anointing that God has for your life and when He says, "move," do it.

2. **Listen to other godly people to help identify your gifts**. If others continually tell you that you would be a great teacher, artist or administrator, listen to them. God often uses people to confirm what is already in our heart. Others may be aware we have a gift before we realize we have that gift. When you're continually complimented in some area, pay attention. That is a strength God has given you to serve others. If others say your cookies are great, get busy baking! How can that be a ministry? There are many shut-ins and homeless people who need the touch of Jesus, and cookies can be a great ministry to those in need.

3. **Write your vision down**. Proverbs 29 says, "Where there is no vision, the people perish." Sitting with folded arms and "waiting on God" to send one thousand signs before we move in our purpose is not what God has in mind. While our vision may not turn out exactly like it looks on paper, it's a great place to start. Offer your vision to God and instead of asking Him to bless *your* plans, tell Him to alter that vision in any way *He* sees fit to help you fulfill the purpose for which you were designed.

4. **Make a list of your strengths**. Are you strong in the arts? Writing? Administration? If you can't identify your strengths, ask others to help you, and write down their responses. God has gifted us with strengths to fulfill our purpose. If your strength is hospitality, you

would not enjoy serving behind a desk where you don't interact with others. You are the "party" person in the Kingdom of God so interacting with people is your strength.

Some of you know your platform well. You have multiple gifts and finding your lane is not the problem. Knowing which lane to drive in is your concern. You teach Sunday school, cook for the sick, serve in Sunday night youth meetings and sing in the choir. You're exhausted, but "bless God," you are using your gifts.

If you're "exhausted" from serving in all of your gifts, perhaps you should get alone with God and ask Him to help balance your life. We cannot be "all things" to "all people." That's why it's so important that we all use our gifts. Too many times the same people are asked to do everything while others sit on the sidelines and benefit from the work of the exhausted. If you're feeling burned out, ask the Lord to provide others who may be waiting "in the wings" to do the job you are weary of doing, then step aside, and make room for them to serve.

5. **Be disciplined**. We often pursue our purpose with passion only to find, over time, that our purpose loses its thrill. Just as anything else in life that's worth having, fulfilling our purpose is hard work. I jokingly tell people that for years, I quit ministry every Monday. Why? Because ministry is hard! We *all* have a ministry and as we pursue that ministry, it's hard physically, emotionally and spiritually. Let me be perfectly clear.

Satan HATES your ministry. That's right. There is absolutely NOTHING about your ministry that he likes and he will do whatever he must do to deter you from fulfilling your purpose in that ministry calling. The good news? We can be disciplined enough to defeat him in the ring. The book of Ephesians says PUT ON the armor of God. This is not an option if you want to succeed in your calling and ministry. The first place Satan often attacks once we allow God to work His purpose in our lives is between our ears. "You didn't really hear from God. Who do you think you are? They're going to laugh at you. You'd better quit while you're ahead." Those are all lies. I have heard them too. Satan's a liar, and he whispers the same lies over and over. Our job is to be so well-fitted in our armor that we know his tactics and how to defeat them. Be disciplined in the work you are called to do, and be disciplined enough to get suited for the fight on a daily basis. If you want to walk in your purpose, there is no plan B.

When we pray for God to show us His purpose for this season of our life, He will do it. He will send the right people, the right places and the provision for His purpose because He has put His symbol on you. Thank Him for your purpose and then serve Him with your "whole heart."

In closing, I challenge you to fulfill the command of the great commission as you live out your specific purpose for the Kingdom. As John Wesley said, "I want the whole Christ for my Savior, the whole Bible for my book, the whole Church for my fellowship, and the whole world for my mission field."

ABOUT THE AUTHOR

Described by one conference attendee as "a cross between comedian Chonda Pierce and Bible teacher Beth Moore," Shannon Perry has been named the favorite speaker by numerous women's conferences and groups. She hosts a weekly TV show, *Grace in High Heels*, which airs on five television networks into over 100 million homes.

She is the author of *"Grace in High Heels: Real Life Reflections of Humor, Hope and Healing"*, *"The Overlooked Generation: Parenting Teens and Tweens in a Complicated Culture"* (endorsed by renowned author and youth evangelist, Josh McDowell), and the Reader's Favorite Award winning book, "*Stand: Staying Balanced with Answers for Real Teen Life.*" She holds a Master's degree in Education and Counseling and is a Certified Instructor in Parenting Classes and Crisis Counseling. She is considered one of the foremost experts on bullying in the country. Her articles have appeared in several magazines and websites including *Focus on the Family* magazine, *Brio* magazine, *Charisma* magazine, *Crosswalk.com*, *iBelieve.com*, *Beliefnet.com*, among many others.

As a singer and songwriter, Shannon has teamed with Lifeway's Songwriter of the Year, Paul Marino, to write and record songs for one full-length CD as well as the song, "Overlooked," featured on Shannon's latest CD, ***In Her Shoes.*** The music video for "Overlooked" was directed by Telly Award-winning filmmaker Jeff Kubach whose credits include the hit television shows *Survivor* and *Burn Notice*. Shannon has performed with the Houston Symphony, at Carnegie Hall, and sang the National Anthem at Houston Astros games and for a Houston Texans NFL game before 70,000 fans.

Shannon has created several original women's conferences, and speaks at churches, retreats, and schools across America. She hosts a radio show, and has been a featured speaker at Salem Radio community events in various cities throughout the country. Visit http://www.ShannonPerry.com for more information.

OTHER BOOKS BY SHANNON PERRY

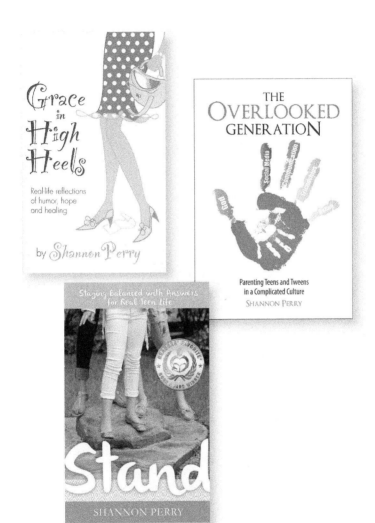

Available at www.ShannonPerry.com

Morgan James
Speakers Group

We connect Morgan James published
authors with live and online events
and audiences who will benefit
from their expertise.